Michael /
You are a good
friend and valued
colleague. Wishing you
the world's best value
in always.
Best Regards,
Rob

# *World's Best Value*™

## *Global Competition in the Information Age*

By Rob Faw

*World's Best Value*™ Global Competition in the Information Age

ISBN #0-9677677-0-9

**To learn more about how to provide *World's Best Value*™ products and services visit www.worldsbestvalue.com.**

*Book design by The Mallard Group, Inc.*

A portion of the proceeds from this book will be donated to Investech Foundation, a charitable-giving company.

# Contents

## Chapter 3 - So You Want To Be a Market Leader

## Chapter 4 - Customer Satisfaction is Everything

## Chapter 5 - Do We Really Hear Our Customers?

## Chapter 6 - Perception is Reality

## Table of Contents

## Table of Contents

# *Acknowledgements*

I want to thank my wife Jill, and my sons Joe and Tommy for their love and support. Their goodness and relationships with their friends, family and community is a source of daily inspiration for me.

During the past few years, writing this book has been a labor of love. It all began on a trans-pacific flight from Seoul, Korea to Los Angeles and continued on trains, planes and hotel rooms during my business travels. It has been an opportunity for me to share my thinking on important personal development and business topics, as well as to learn and develop myself during the process. There have been countless contributions to the creation of ***World's Best Value*™ – Global Competition in the Information Age**. I would like to especially thank Karl Fulk and Bill Wiard for their time and literary support of this effort.

During the past 20 years, I have been privileged to meet so many good people in the communications industry. It is my hope and prayer that people and companies around the world accept their leadership responsibilities and constantly strive to create ***World's Best Value*™** businesses.

I have been blessed to know a number of people who are making a difference in the world and have been valuable mentors and coaches for me. I would like to thank Otto Berlin, Oscar Carignan, Rich Fulk, Bob Gaynor and Gary Seamans for taking the time to care about me and my development as a person and business leader.

## World's Best Value™

It is only right to acknowledge people like John Chambers of Cisco, Bill Gates of Microsoft, Jack Welch of General Electric, Rich McGinn of Lucent Technologies, Carley Fiorina of Hewlett Packard, John Roth of Nortel Networks, Jacques Nasser of Ford, Steve Case of America On Line, Michael Dell of Dell Computer, Jerry Yang of Yahoo, and Chris Galvin of Motorola. These people and many others are taking a leadership position in building *World's Best Value™* companies. As leaders, they share their time and thoughts about business and their own companies, providing rich perspectives for those who care to listen and understand.

I want to acknowledge all of my business associates, customers and partners during my career at Paradyne, AT&T, Westell, Atlantech Technologies, Sedona Networks and Virtual Access. The original Westell INternational ("WIN") team was very special. I want to recognize all of those people at Westell who chose to follow a dream of building a business that could change the world. The WIN leadership team included Manuel Andrade, Michael Clegg, Dave Corey, Mike Day, Joseph Elchakieh, Ron Koval and Paula Uselis. Greg Bella, Kurt Bradtmueller, Richard Carter, Brian Henrichs, Lori Ritterskamp, Bill Rodey and Kevin Steffey helped realize the dream. All of my colleagues are valued friends and I appreciate their many contributions to the communications industry.

I want to share a final thought about *World's Best Value™ - Global Competition in the Information Age*; the teachings from this book have application for start-up companies as well as Fortune 500 global corporations. *World's Best Value™* businesses can be found

xii

## *Acknowledgements*

everywhere. I would like to acknowledge all those people, present and future, who are taking the time to be the best in the world at what they do. You have a terrific responsibility that goes along with your good fortune, and I have every confidence you will be successful.

# *Introduction*

What in the world is happening in today's global economy? The Information Age is causing businesses around the world to change their size and scope at a startling pace.

British Telecom is reducing the size of its work force in half. Bell Atlantic has acquired NYNEX and is merging with GTE. SBC has absorbed Pacific Bell and Ameritech. MCIWorldCom is on a worldwide buying spree and is merging with Sprint. Soon, the former seven Regional Bell Operating Companies in the United States will be three or four companies providing local, long distance and international service offerings.

The rate of change in most industries is challenging companies to re-think their business strategies and causing a leadership renewal in search for spiritual meaning.

Whole industries are converging as governments debate the merits and strategic importance of the Information Age. Business-to-business on-line commerce is projected to soar from $43 billion to $1 trillion by 2003. The Internet is changing everything with more than 80 million people in the United States on-line in 1999!

Have you ever sat in a meeting and someone asked the question, "What does world-class mean?" In athletic competition, it is easy to measure. We have the World Cup in soccer, the Olympics, and international athletic events such as track and field. All provide a barometer for the best competitors to determine who can be considered world-class. But in the business world, how would anyone know if they found a world-class company?

## World's Best Value™

There is business competition, and it's conducted on a global basis. However, winning and losing is difficult to measure due to the complexity of bringing together diverse groups of people, systems and processes. Stock markets can be an indicator, but even for all its complexity, the stock market does not measure beyond stockholder value.

How about strategic planning? In the 1990s America On Line focused its strategy on creating a community of users with little regard to near-term financial results and vaulted past pioneers Prodigy and CompuServe. For many companies, however, strategic planning is a financially driven exercise that bears no resemblance to the reality of the marketplace. In many cases, it has become an annual rethinking about tactics for next year's financial targets, as opposed to assessing the critical conditions for success necessary to compete and succeed in a global marketplace. Prior to the wide-scale competitive threats from start-up companies and globalization of businesses, companies could afford to focus just on revenue growth from existing markets.

There are companies that are well known for the creation of new products and services that customers want, at the price they want and at a time that meets their customer requirements. Motorola, for example, has announced an intention to develop travel automation software for two-way wireless communications for business travelers. When was the last time a company had a shared vision of what it means to be the best in the world in time to market or *Cycle Time?*

My conclusion is that companies that are universally recognized as world-class are best in class in cycle time development of new products.  They have a daily passion in pursuit of fast product development cycle time as a key competitive differentiator. Sony, Microsoft, Intel, Nokia, Cisco Systems, FedEx and MCIWorldCom, for example, all know how to get products and services to market as fast or faster than their worldwide competitors.

*World's Best Value™* is a simplification of complex business system perspectives.  *World's Best Value™* is a guidepost for business survival and long-term success.  So many of our world's business leaders, managers and employees at all levels are working very hard without knowing their destination.  The relentless pursuit of *activities* as opposed to *outcomes* can cause companies to be the best they can be, only nobody wants what they have.  In the 21$^{st}$ century, winning companies and people will be those who stay ahead of the change curve.  They will constantly redefine their industries and create new markets by challenging the status quo.  These 21$^{st}$ century people and businesses will reinvent the competitive landscape.

*World's Best Value™* can mean different things to different people.  For customers in highly competitive (most) industries, *World's Best Value™* means the availability of world-class quality products and services at a price that makes the customer successful.

Customers want to work with a supplier who consistently and passionately works at being the best partner/supplier compared to any other business in the world.  Every interaction by these businesses with their customers adds value.  Every transaction between people and groups of people within these companies is predicated on adding value for the customers.

*World's Best Value™* companies are like leaders. Steven Covey describes the paradigm shift from *management* to one of *principle-centered leadership*. Leaders develop, contribute and make a difference in the lives of their employees, community, customers, and shareowners — each and every day. Leaders are not found everywhere, but countless numbers are in pursuit of an excellence leading towards *World's Best Value™*.

If you care about your customers, fellow workers, company and your job; ask the question, *"What is our company doing to be world-class and provide World's Best Value™ products and services for our customers?"*

Imagine fierce competition in a global economy and equally or greater skilled workers and companies around the corner or half-way around the world. Yahoo, for example, has some 200 employees who search the Internet daily to benchmark competitor websites and continuously improve their own product and service offerings. Competitors around the corner or around the world are continually planning and executing their strategy to take customers and market share away from your business. Imagine not being able to provide wealth creation for your investors. Imagine not being profitable, successful or developing your business as a market leader. Imagine being unemployed because your competitors create new jobs elsewhere and dominate whole industries. Global competition is a matter of survival!

Each of us can gain collective insight and meaningful understanding of what it means to compete when our lives are at stake. We can learn what customers really want in a global marketplace. Despite the recent Asian, Russian and Latin American economic crises, stock market fluctuations and on-going world-wide economic challenges, companies are weathering the storm and growing stronger from competition. These companies know how to provide *World's Best Value™* and compete in the global economy. We should expect *World's Best Value™* from businesses, governments, education institutions and all organizations.

# Chapter 1

## Characteristics of *World's Best Value*™

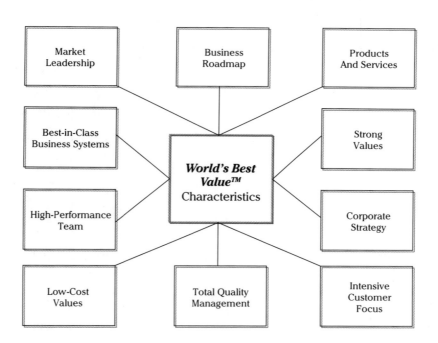

## Characteristics of World's Best Value™

**World's Best Value™** is a potentially complex business concept but yet quite simple when considered from a business system perspective. **World's Best Value™** is being the best in the world and being perceived that way by your employees, customers, shareowners and community. *Michael Porter*, author of *Competitive Advantage,* describes that successful companies in the 21$^{st}$ century must have a goal for learning and connection with business strategy.

It is impossible to provide **World's Best Value™** without understanding everything there is to know about your customers, your competition and your own business. All employees must share this understanding. If there is incomplete knowledge, it is difficult to add value at every level in the business. And just when you think you have found it, everything changes!

The laws of physics describe a phenomenon known as the *Chaos Theory.* It suggests that when a butterfly flaps its wings in the Philippines, it can cause a hurricane in the South Atlantic Ocean. Chaos Theory says there is a relationship between every molecule of air on the planet. It is exciting, but kind-of frightening. In a *business system* there is also a relationship between everything within that system, known and unknown.

**World's Best Value™** is being the best in the world at understanding those relationships and translating them into sustainable value for your customers. **World's Best Value™** can be described as a science and an art. It is human relationships and it is software. It is financial strength and process discipline. It is *unlocking the human potential.*

3

## World's Best Value™

Knowledge with understanding adds value, and it is just one element or characteristic of **World's Best Value™**. What follows is a set of characteristics found in companies that provide **World's Best Value™**:

 ### World-class products and services

In order to play the game of global competition it is essential that companies have products and services that meet customer needs. Products and services must have some intrinsic value that cannot be duplicated by any other company in the world. Products and services must be world-class if businesses are to survive in the long term. Short-term success from first to market can provide value and differentiation, but in the long run there will be competition, and survival is at stake.

The communications industry (telecommunications and data communications service providers and equipment suppliers) is the world's second largest industry behind the automobile industry. By 2003, an estimated 600 million personal computers will be competing with two billion networked, hand-held devices, intelligent cell phones, household appliances, vending machines and television set top boxes, all connected to the Internet.

What is the world going to look like when there is ever-increasing competition in the communications industry? What are the implications for competition and convergence when the communications industry becomes the world's largest industry early next century? What will the competitive environment be

4

when regulatory authorities actively promote deregulation and competition, defining our industries and transforming the way we do business? The United States is forging ahead with widespread use and limited regulation of the Internet, thus promoting e-commerce activities. Individual countries outside of the United States are following the U.S. lead in e-commerce. British Telecom, for example, has recently moved to cut the cost of Internet access to speed up e-commerce. It seems that Europe, however, may be slower in the uptake of e-commerce as cross border shopping could get caught up in a legal tangle as a result of changes to international law agreements between member countries.

Like the computer industry in the 1980s, the communications industry in the new millennium can look forward to dramatic price erosion and increasing product quality in an environment of huge technology shifts. Optical networking, for instance, is expected to grow to $10 billion in 2002. The $225 billion telecommunications-equipment market is growing 50 percent annually and a $25 billion data-networking market is growing at an estimated 15 percent per year. The key differentiators between success and failure in the Information Age will be the people and companies that provide *World's Best Value™*.

The entertainment industry continues to grow and change. Seagram's, the whisky people, who own Time Warner, the movies people, are restructuring their distribution strategy to become cable and broadcast TV (distribution) people. *World's Best Value™* companies are already thinking about the next 20 years and restructuring the world they live in.

## World's Best Value™

The automobile industry is shifting and churning as well. Ford Motor is centralizing it's product management functions and has a vision of being one of the best global companies in the world. It has acquired competitors such as Volvo and Jaguar and at the same time is fiercely cutting costs and streamlining operations. Ford wants to be a powerful growth-oriented company that competes against what it expects will be just a few global competitors.

Daewoo, the consumer electronics company in Korea, has entered the automobile manufacturing business because their long-term view of the world is that cars will be comprised of more than 50% electronic components in the 21st century. The rules of the game are changing, and the only key to success and survival is to provide *World's Best Value™* .

Is it our imagination, or do UPS and FedEx dominate the world's small package courier business? Remember in the early 1980's, TNT of Australia was rapidly expanding on a worldwide basis and considered to be world-class? TNT is a fine company and serves a lot of customers, but they are losing market share. Every day market leaders are competing to dominate the small package distribution business and delivering *World's Best Value™* products and services.

Products and services have to be world-class, highest quality, lowest relative cost and highest performance standards. Customers who seek *World's Best Value™* from their suppliers and partners will only structure their business around *World's Best Value™* companies. Otherwise, low price wins and every product

6

and every service in every industry becomes a commodity.

---

*The 1ˢᵗ characteristic of a **World's Best Value™***
*company is choice of market segment and*
*providing world-class products and services*

---

 **Best practices, business and information systems**

It is often the case that information technology companies are the worst offenders in under-utilizing information technologies. Business growth usually strains their ability to manage and grow internal information systems capabilities. All world-class businesses that consistently add value to their customers, began thinking about information systems at the time of inception. Hewlett Packard, for example, has an information system that answers every e-mail message it receives from customers. Business and information systems were critical elements of HP's strategic intent.

Dave Rungee, author of *Telecommunications for Competitive Advantage*, compares the use of quality business and information systems as being the lifeblood of not only a company's business, but also its customers' businesses. He describes business and information systems as electronic drugs for a sick patient. You can't live without them!

While the capacity of the human spirit is seemingly unlimited, only so many arms and legs can be thrown at solving business issues for customers. People need tools. Every major corporation is either in the process of, or has completed, the re-engi-

7

neering of their businesses. Today's re-engineering efforts are nothing more than yesterday's lack of planning!

McKinsey and Company, Andersen Consulting and others would be glad to provide (for a fee) a summary of best practices for business and information systems. Shining examples of best practices for business and information systems include FedEx, American Airlines and Saturn Car Company. Best practices boil down to disciplined, sustainable, well-understood and documented business practices that provide guidelines for *good people to do great things* for their customers. Business processes would need to follow electronic information systems and vice versa.

Many companies unfortunately have such convoluted information system strategies; they spend all of their time trying to set up systems for existing practices that do not serve customers. World-class companies establish information systems and business practices that serve the needs of their customers first, and then work backwards! With the right vision and capabilities, emerging entrants in any industry can leapfrog established corporations who have heritage business practices that are out of date. Critical mass and legacy information systems for larger companies in this environment can become a liability.

Customers may not always know what their suppliers of products and services are doing with their information systems and business practices. Customers love any supplier that develops seamless information systems and business practices which add value.

---

*The 2ⁿᵈ characteristic of a **World's Best Value™** company is implementation and use of business processes and information systems that are best practice in any industry*

---

 ### High-performance team members

I have never met a person who wakes up in the morning, goes to work and says how he or she wants to do a *bad* job on that day! There are, however, people around the world who believe that companies owe them a living. In addition, many people believe that society owes them a living. These same people, as employees of any company, are so focused on their own wants and needs that it is impossible for them to consider reaching out and giving all that they can give to serve an external customer.

What is the social responsibility of a company to its employees? Why do many people not take advantage of company provided and sponsored education and training programs? People who invest in themselves are developing their potential and capacity to serve customers. If the global economy creates a battlefield for whole nations to cooperate and compete, why would anyone believe that yesterday's talents will meet tomorrow's customer requirements?

Small entrepreneurial companies seem to have an advantage because they are creating their businesses from scratch and can hand select people who wish to follow a common vision. History books are littered with examples of companies that never scaled. The management teams never invested in themselves and never stuck around to find out if their company actually provided value in a global economy.

Whatever happened to Wang, Commodore Computers and countless other companies that had leadership positions in growth markets? These companies were slow to invest in their people and businesses when technology shifts created new business opportunities. Companies and people need to invest in themselves! FedEx, for example, invests three percent of total operating expenses into training, or six times the proportion of most companies. People have to be the best in the world in order to contribute in the global economy. Training, education, motivation and dedication are all attributes of high-performance people. Not everyone wants to change the world, but just about everyone would rather be successful than unsuccessful. High-performance people have a tendency to seek balance in every aspect of their lives and are the fuel and driving force behind companies that provide *World's Best Value™* products and services.

---

*The 3ʳᵈ characteristic of a **World's Best Value™** company is high-performance people who develop themselves and serve customers*

---

 **Low-cost values**

Another attribute of *World's Best Value™* companies is they have a value system of low cost. Low cost does not mean cheap. Low cost means thinking about judicious investments in people, processes and business operations in pursuit of serving customers. Most customers are not willing to pay your company to maintain top of the line accommodations or first class travel. Most customers are not willing to fund research and development projects that do not relate to the overall business strategy.

*World's Best Value™* companies constantly think about how much they are spending on their people and the operating expenses required to serve their customers. There is no right answer regarding low cost other than to ensure costs of operations directly relate to adding value for customers.

Let's consider some questions that provide vivid examples of what organizations can ask to determine if they are knowingly or unknowingly providing low-cost values for customers:

1) Is consideration given to the cost/benefit of staffing?
2) Does the quality of new employees make others better?
3) Is consideration given to growth potential of new employees?
4) Do employees have the capacity to grow with the business?
5) Do employees spend company resources as if their own?
6) Do information systems increase the capacity to serve customers?
7) Do employees seek balance in order to INCREASE output?
8) Are there financial limitations for professional development?
9) Is there an environment of low cost values?
10) Are low cost values understood?

---

*The 4ᵗʰ characteristic of a **World's Best Value™** company
is a culture of low cost values that includes employee
development, productivity and operating efficiency*

---

 *Total quality management culture*

Total Quality Management (TQM) considers all aspects of quality practices, process improvement and organizational alignment. In many companies outside of Japan, TQM is unfortunately treated as a program and not always a way of doing business. Western culture has not grown up with the understanding of providing quality in every transaction with internal and external customers. Noted exceptions such as Ford, Hewlett Packard and Motorola have made significant strides through intensive training and development of measurement systems.

TQM in fact needs to be a way of life at the senior executive level of every **World's Best Value™** organization. Executives must set the tone and make the necessary resources available to help create and nurture a TQM culture. Much has been written about Dr. Edward Deming, who is recognized as the quality Godfather throughout the world. It is well worth learning more about Deming and his quality principles.

A TQM culture is often a different culture for many companies. When TQM is implemented in a business, significant change management activities are necessary in order to create the right kind of cultural framework to produce the desired TQM outcome. Nirvana in TQM companies usually creates a statistical measurement system that considers variables related to customer

12

satisfaction. Many organizations find it very difficult to create a total customer satisfaction index.

Indices such as profit improvement, defects in parts per million, customer ship date defects, returned goods, warranty repair, cycle time improvement, customer satisfaction and employee satisfaction surveys usually are found in overall TQM measurements.

An important part of TQM is *Hoshin Planning*. Hoshin planning, as defined by the Japanese, is a simple strategic planning tool. A key responsibility for any Chief Executive Officer in a TQM company is to help define the *vision* and *mission* of the company. In a **World's Best Value™** company, Hoshin planning is about PRIORITY planning. In a **World's Best Value™** company, Hoshin plans become **World's Best Value™** plans and should not be created in a vacuum since the top priorities provide the impetus for each and every person to set his or her individual priorities. In a perfectly planned TQM organization, every strategy, every objective, and every business initiative in the company will relate back to **World's Best Value™** planning or top priorities. It is usually expressed as no more than 10 priorities. One can only imagine the power, focus and synergy in any organization that practices **World's Best Value™** planning. Customers expect such a culture in a **World's Best Value™** company.

---

*The 5th characteristic of a **World's Best Value™***
*company is a TQM culture with a commitment*
*by the leadership and all employees*

---

## World's Best Value™

 ### Intensive global customer focus

**World's Best Value™** companies must be able to operate in an environment of global competition. Their customers are often found throughout the world. Industry influencers such as *Peter Senge, Warren Bennis and John Naisbitt* have written about the attributes of a global corporation. This topic has widespread interest because so many companies are in constant pursuit of global success.

Shared global values, strategies and business practices, acted upon in local economies, are attributes of truly global corporations. Respect for cultural differences while maintaining common corporate values is a consistent characteristic of companies that have an intensive global customer focus.

Imagine the value provided to a customer anywhere in the world, where an employee can draw upon global resources. Ford, for example, is planning a structural shakeup in the 21$^{st}$ century that will give executives more responsibility over car brands and marketing. They are pushing all employees to get closer to the customer and investing in innovative new ventures like Microsoft Network's CarPoint web site. Further, Ford is creating network exchanges for suppliers to create large-scale business-to-business electronic commerce to handle the billions of transactions a year with their worldwide suppliers.

Intensive global customer focus is very easy to describe and often difficult to implement. Global shared values can be confused with country and regional cultural differences. Every business leader, in every company around the world, wants to provide value for their customer and each believes they know how best to provide that value. Have you ever seen or been part of a global corporation that has as many mission statements and value systems as they do operating business units or countries in which they do business? Intensive global customer focus can only be created centrally in the form of corporate guidelines, universally applicable values and world-class communications systems. Imagine a world where a sales executive in Sao Paulo, Brazil learns from a colleague in London, England and provides global insights, understanding and solutions that meet customer requirements. That kind of intensive global customer focus would be powerful!

---

*The 6th Characteristic of a **World's Best Value™**
company is an intensive desire and focus to
serve customers on a global basis*

---

 *Principle centered leadership*

There has been so much written about the topic of leadership throughout the ages. Leadership has as much to do with philosophy as it does with management practices. It has as much to do with *Aristotle,* as it has to do with *Peter Drucker*. Leadership is as much of a feeling as it is a practice. It is as much an art as it is a science. Leaders often take stands in the spirit of what is right. They really do not pay attention to the prevailing school of thought or behavior unless it is the right thing. Every great book written about leadership describes an out-of-this-world passion or spiritual theme. Leadership is about a belief system that constantly challenges the edge of capabilities and competencies of people. There is an air of leadership throughout **World's Best Value™** companies. Leadership must be recognized and valued as a key differentiator. Customers will recognize leadership in a company without even asking!

The book, *Principle Centered Leadership and The Seven Habits of Highly Effective Leaders*, written by *Stephen R. Covey*, captures some of the very best research, insight and understanding about leadership and how it relates to people. It's doctrine can be applied to each and every person. In fact, given its worldwide acceptance and practice, *The Seven Habits of Highly Effective Leaders* is one of the most widely adopted books on leadership. *The Seven Habits of Highly Effective Leaders* has sold nearly 13 million copies since it was first published in 1989.

Imagine the possibilities to serve customers if each and every person thinks and acts as a leader when they interact with customers. Think of the value provided. *Dr. Covey* describes the seven habits as (1) Be proactive (2) Begin with the end in mind (3) Put first things first (4) Think win - win (5) Seek first to understand then to be understood (6) Synergize and (7) Sharpen the saw. These habits can be found or developed in everyone. *The Seven Habits of Highly Effective Leaders* has special meaning and further study would be required in order to internalize their power and application. *The Seven Habits of Highly Effective Leaders* relates to maturity of people over time and looks at dependence, independence and interdependence as the continuum of personal development and success.

### Characteristics of World's Best Value™

I have had the opportunity to help create a Principle Centered Leadership culture in large global corporations, medium-size multinational businesses and start-up companies. For instance, at Westell INternational, each employee received formal training, and *Principle Centered Leadership* became part of the cultural foundation to serve worldwide customers. We also extended *Principle Centered Leadership* to our partner relationships around the world. We developed the business from no products with no customers and no distribution channels to operations in over 50 countries and a profitable $20 million worldwide business. Our achievements were accomplished in less than three years and played an important part in our parent company going public! *Principle Centered Leadership* was one of the keys to our success.

*Principle Centered Leadership* works, it is powerful, and it is based on fundamental truths and values that stand the test of time. It is based around people and trusting relationships. Imagine a company with trust at every level; with customers, shareowners and the community. Customers and competitors will recognize any company that builds a culture around strong values and belief systems like *Principle Centered Leadership* as a **World's Best Value™** company. A *Principle Centered Leadership* culture of any organization applies to every person at every level in the business.

---

*The 7ᵗʰ characteristic of a **World's Best Value™** company is
a culture built on strong values and belief systems
such as Principle Centered Leadership*

---

17

# *World's Best Value*™ **Plan**
## Characteristics of *World's Best Value*™

Objective: Identify the characteristics of a *World's Best Value*™ company.

Priorities:

1) Determine market segment and focus on leadership.

2) Produce world-class products and services.

3) Implement best in class business processes.

4) Implement best in class information systems.

5) Build and invest in a high-performance team.

6) Develop a low-cost values culture.

7) Develop a total quality management culture.

8) Create an intensive focus to serve customers globally.

9) Build a culture of strong values and belief systems.

10) Develop and communicate a well understood strategy.

# Chapter 2

## Going Global for Competitive Survival

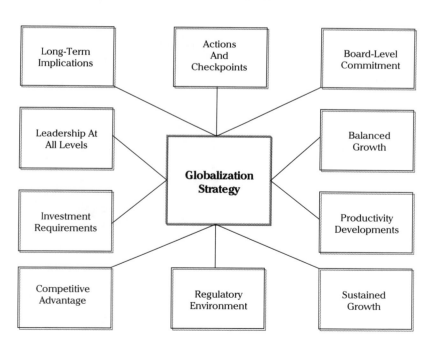

Long-Term Implications

Actions And Checkpoints

Board-Level Commitment

Leadership At All Levels

Globalization Strategy

Balanced Growth

Investment Requirements

Productivity Developments

Competitive Advantage

Regulatory Environment

Sustained Growth

## Going Global for Competitive Survival

 *Globalization strategy*

My experience and research shows that a company should not start or maintain a business on a global basis without a globalization strategy. For example, in the 1980s, Hayes Modems was a worldwide leader in modem technology. During the 1990s the company was not able to effectively compete in developing new digital communications technologies, nor did it have a globalization plan. Both issues resulted in Hayes filing for bankruptcy in 1999. An incomplete globalization strategy will result in the misuse of time and resources.

There are numerous examples of leaders who have successful global businesses such as Rupert Murdoch of the News Corporation and Lou Gerstner of IBM. Jack Welch of General Electric and his leadership team have figured out the globalization model and execute it every day. It is tempting, but risky, to start a globalization strategy with a single success in one country and incrementally growing the business in other countries. This can be a flawed strategy that follows the creation of a multinational business that is not always scalable. Globalization is a process driven by the fall of communism and explosion of knowledge-based businesses and instant communication as well as availability of information and capital.

## World's Best Value™

There is a simple set of questions that can be asked in order to critically assess the globalization strategy of any company. A globalization strategy needs to answer the following:

1) What is the size of the total marketplace?
2) What is the available market?
3) What is the distribution strategy?
4) What is the product strategy?
5) Who is the competition?
6) What are the barriers to entry?
7) What is the regulatory environment?
8) What are the investment requirements?
9) What acquisitions are necessary to gain market share?
10) What are the long-term financial projections?

Globalization strategy does not mean multinational, unless that is the chosen strategy. Globalization means operating on a worldwide basis as if your company is a local business. Multinational means providing goods and services to customers that are headquartered in one part of the world but operate in others. Multinational strategies are typically very limited in their scope. AT&T, for instance, in the late 1980s had a multinational strategy that provided telecommunication and data communication services to their largest U.S.-based customers.

In the 1980s, AT&T struggled with globalization requirements and was somewhat confused about harnessing the business growth potential outside of the United States. Today, AT&T is forming an alliance to service its global customers and buying up cable companies with plans to offer telephone, cable, TV and Internet services to consumers. The mergers with Tele-Communications Inc. and Media One are worth more than $110 billion and provide AT&T with access to 17 million cable consumers in the United States. In addition, AT&T will spend an estimated $7 billion upgrading the newly acquired cable networks.

While Wall Street is skeptical of AT&T's strategy, ultimately, their chief executive officer, Michael Armstrong must create a global strategy. He must create a range of business alliances that positions AT&T for worldwide business growth and success.

Globalization strategies enable companies to expand revenues and profits and manage economic fluctuations that can occur in different countries or regions. Global risk management is more challenging, as the worldwide economy becomes more globally interdependent. Gillette, Coca-Cola, IBM, Merck and McDonald's are good examples of companies that have staked out the world as their marketplace and diligently work their globalization strategies for the benefit of their customers, employees, shareowners and communities.

*Going global* is a matter of competitive survival. Globalization is measured in years, decades or centuries, and as the saying goes, *only the strong survive*! Businesses that operate in a particular city, in a county or province, or in a particular state or country, should always keep in mind that competitors may be out of sight, in a neighboring county or city or state. Going global does not always have to mean halfway around the world. I was recently in a meeting with a business colleague in Ottawa, Canada, and the topic of conversation was about corporate survival. After quite a lengthy discussion and analysis, we concluded that corporate survival is a systems level issue and similar to human survival. There are no guarantees!

---

*A globalization strategy is essential for long-term success and competitive survival*

---

 ### *Going global, a model*

If you are going to take your company global or if you already do business on a global basis, a model for understanding and communications is essential. It is challenging enough to get the strategy right. It is another level of detail to widely communicate the strategy so it is in the hearts and the minds of all employees. A simple model can take the complexity out of doing business on a worldwide basis.

Remember the questions we asked earlier? Those are the same questions that should be answered as part of a globalization strategy and they will form the basis for a working business model. An interrelationship model or simple flow chart can be used.

# *Going Global for Competitive Survival*

## Globalization Business Model

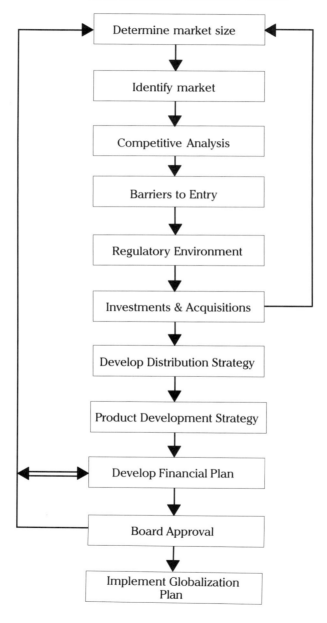

### Board Level Commitment

How many businesses have developed global expansion plans only to have them reversed six months or a year into the investment? Chief Executive Officers and business leaders at all levels must ensure that globalization activities are understood and supported at the highest levels within a company. For public and many privately-held companies, this is almost always the board of directors. Doing business outside of familiar surroundings or business borders requires support from those who have fiduciary responsibility for the well-being of a corporation. CMG, the Information Technology consultancy, reported boards that do not understand e-commerce hold back more than twenty five percent of executives who try to implement electronic commerce solutions.

Beware of the non-executive board member who says, *"we have enough business opportunity here in the good old United States!"* That kind of reaction to a globalization strategy is based on either ignorance or lack of experience. It is not unusual for patriotic prejudices to surface when dealing with the unknown and unfamiliar. It is better to get the issues out on the table and deal with them as a leadership team that includes management and the board of directors.

*World's Best Value™* companies have a board constituency that is made up of seasoned international executives. Diversity is absolutely required in order to maintain and maximize shareowner interests. *World's Best Value™* companies typically do not want non-executives to be learning about globalization at periodic board meetings. On the job training for board members is not a luxury that *World's Best Value™* companies can afford.

In order to increase shareowner value, Disney, Citigroup, Warner–Lambert and Microsoft have diversity on their boards and actively seek and understand business opportunities outside of their home country. Sony, Toyota, British Airways and Alcatel are also good examples.

---

*Sustaining a long-term global strategy in*
*World's Best Value™ companies requires board level*
*understanding, support and commitment*

---

 *Strategy development*

The development of globalization plans must include leaders who will be responsible for implementation. The plans are usually complex enough that diverse groups of managers and employees of a company are required to provide the necessary leadership for value creation. I like the model of putting a strategy *stake in the ground* in order to provide context and framework. The key to this stake in the ground practice is to be careful not to defend the initial stake in the ground as the strategy answer, but rather use it as a vehicle for input, support and commitment from people at all levels.

### *World's Best Value™*

Strategy development is actually pretty straightforward. It takes energy, commitment and resolve to deal with the business and cultural differences that naturally arise. A model that I've used successfully is as follows:

1) Find the champion that will drive the process.
2) Assemble a small team to create the initial strategy.
3) Follow the 80/20 rule to answer the important questions.
4) Don't let research get in the way of the obvious solutions.
5) Circulate the first draft of the globalization plan.
6) Secure written and verbal feedback on the plan.
7) Circulate the second draft of the globalization plan.
8) Include financial projections in second draft.
9) Edit final draft with CEO and CFO for input and support.
10) Executive sponsor support for board presentation.

A globalization strategy needs to be one of the top three priorities set by the chief executive officer and board in order to be successful. If a globalization strategy takes longer than two to three months to develop, it very likely is not viewed as a priority or the skilled resources are not in your company to champion and implement the globalization initiative. A champion and dedicated team can do anything in two to three months given the right support and resources to complete a globalization plan.

---

*Strategy Development is an essential ingredient for long-term sustainable success for **World's Best Value™** companies*

---

## *Going Global for Competitive Survival*

 ### *Investments and resources for success*

I once asked the CEO of a publicly traded networking company what was the key responsibility of being a chief executive? He thought about it for just a brief minute and said it is nothing more than the *allocation of financial and human resources*. Over the years I've reflected on those words and, while I understand being a CEO is more than allocation of resources, it is a big part of the job. The same is true for globalization strategies. What are the investments and resources required to be successful? Microsoft thinks it is its annual $3 billion research and investment in software.

Cisco is investing in *"New World Network"* technologies that blend the technology of the Internet with high-speed optical fibers, cable and wireless systems to carry voice and data everywhere. Intel has made investments of more than $5 billion in more than 300 technology companies. Direct investment by U.S. companies in Europe and European companies in the U.S. is valued in excess of $1 trillion. Market leaders are investing heavily in securing their leadership position in the Information Age.

Globalization strategies for many companies can bring out the best and the worst in people and the companies they work for. Company leaders can have an emotionally positive response and absolute commitment to a globalization plan. And over time these same leaders can have a knee-jerk hesitation to provide the necessary investments and resources because of missed expectations and short-term thinking.

Leaders can also find it very difficult to make available the best and brightest people required to grow a business outside any home country. When a company hesitates to provide the necessary resources and investments for global success, it is a warning flag that puts at risk the successful implementation of a globalization plan.

Global corporations such as Coca-Cola would only operate in China or Eastern Europe, for example, with local bottling plants staffed by local nationals. Worldwide business growth requires investments that enable market share creation and value differentiation. Honda and Toyota, for example, have concluded that mass marketing automobiles in the United States requires in-country production. There are countless examples of going global that fall short of full success. There is all too often a strategy to be a global competitor, but implementation falls short because the investments are not made or continued. This is especially true in the communications industry.

Voice and data-communication service providers must create relationships with in-country companies in order to provide a multinational service offering. Similarly, communications and networking equipment suppliers cannot be successful unless they have equipment that is approved to meet local connection standards to the telephone network. The investment model, however, for each is quite different. Service providers tend to have recurring revenue streams and equipment suppliers are dependent on volume equipment sales.

### Going Global for Competitive Survival

Whether you are establishing a brand recognition program for toothpaste in Europe or type approving communications equipment for resale in Latin America, each will have its own investment and resource requirements — each necessary for global success.

---

*A **World's Best Value™** company makes the necessary investments and application of resources to create conditions for global business success*

---

 ### Competitive environment

To go global and provide **World's Best Value™** products and services, companies must understand their competitive environment in great detail. Ten questions to ask regarding the competitive environment are:

1) Who is the primary competitor today?
2) What is the long-term strategy of the competition?
3) Is the industry growing or mature?
4) Will competitors increase investments over time?
5) What specific actions will create market share?
6) What are the barriers to entry for new competitors?
7) Will your competitors merge to create competition?
8) Are skilled resources readily available?
9) What are the long-term competitive trends?
10) What three factors create competitive advantage?

## World's Best Value™

I find it rather amusing when sports franchises and business leaders discount the importance of their competition. How many times have we heard, *"We just need to take care of our own business,"* or, *"I'm not sure we have any real competition as what we do is pretty unique."* This kind of response is so far from the truth, it is either ignorance or naiveté. Start-up companies that focus heavily on technology development can often misread or misunderstand the competitive environment.

Let's take the discussion about understanding the competitive environment to another level — life and death! Does anyone really believe that the greatest military force on the face of the planet, the United States, does not have intelligence about its competition? Can we imagine a military leader of any nation executing a war plan without having some understanding of their competition? Was the Gulf War won in a matter of days because the U.S. armed forces were lucky or strategic? Did they win the war because they were fortunate or skilled in the execution of their battle plan?

***World's Best Value*™** companies understand the value of competitive analysis and use the information for their competitive advantage. What are the product, people, performance and price weaknesses of their competitors? How can those weaknesses be exploited?

---

*A **World's Best Value*™** *company is relentless in its*
*pursuit of understanding competition and creating*
*competitive advantage from that knowledge*

---

## *Going Global for Competitive Survival*

 *Government priorities*

When a **World's Best Value™** company goes global; they have an understanding of the government priorities for countries where they do business. What are the social trends that may influence regulation? What are the tax considerations that must be understood in order to optimize worldwide tax planning? Can investments be made to attract county, state, province or national grants? Are expenditures in use of information technology consistent or inconsistent with government priorities? An understanding of government priorities enables a **World's Best Value™** company to develop and execute corporate strategies that are comprehensive and considerate of not only their corporate objectives, but also how these objectives fit with government priorities.

The United States government actively promotes competition, innovation and lower prices and uses the Federal Trade Commission as its vehicle to enforce this priority. It can, however, become politically motivated, but its priority is intended to be pro-competition. Is Microsoft abusing its monopoly position or competing fairly to provide value to customers? Is the landmark anti-trust case pitting the U.S. government against Microsoft a case of discontinuity with government priorities or just a reflection of a litigious nation seeking new ways to misuse taxpayers' dollars? A prospective break-up of Microsoft may or may not lead to increased competition and benefit the consumer.

Regardless of the answer to these questions, a lesson learned is that Microsoft and any other company seeking to become or maintain itself as a *World's Best Value™* company, must understand government priorities and act accordingly. Otherwise, precious management resources are fighting lawsuits instead of creating value for customers.

---

*A **World's Best Value™** company actively seeks*
*to understand government policy priorities in order*
*to maximize use of corporate resources*

---

 ### Regulatory environment and trends

Most employees do not really understand the regulatory environment, let alone the regulatory trends of that environment. Profits can be made or lost by anticipating and acting upon trends and changes in the regulatory environment.

After 13 years of negotiation, China and the U.S. reached an agreement in 1999 for China to enter the World Trade Organization ("WTO"). Author *John Naisbitt* has predicted the rise of the Asian tiger in his *Megatrends Asia* book. China's entry in the WTO is a bold and risky bet by China that will open up its domestic markets to foreign competition. The 134-nation WTO sets and enforces rules of global commerce. It will require China to dismantle or reduce barriers to protect underachieving, inefficient companies. The impact on China and its people should be dramatic.

*Business Week* reports that Economist *Hu Angange* of the Chinese Academy of Sciences says as many as 10 million jobs will be lost as tariffs that protect wheat and corn growers are reduced. University of California – San Diego economist *Naughton* predicts that the changes resulting from WTO membership will drive Chinese companies to enter into markets that take advantage of its low-cost labor. The worldwide economic implications from China joining the WTO will be determined over the next few decades. ***World's Best Value™*** companies must anticipate and embrace regulatory changes for their own economic benefit.

The Telecommunications Act of 1996 is another prominent example of regulatory legislation that must be well understood. The regulatory environment has enabled thousands of jobs to be created. The Act has also enabled thousands of companies to be created, many funded by venture capital and initial public offerings. The regulatory environment has accelerated the trend towards corporate mergers and consolidation of the Regional Bell Operating Companies ("RBOCs"). Additionally, it has spawned the emergence of Internet Service Providers ("ISPs") and convergence of telecommunications and data-communications industries. The Telecommunications Act of 1996 will go down in history as the single regulatory action that had a life-changing impact on the way the world lives and communicates.

The regulatory trend of communications liberalization is extending to other countries as nations compete for their economic fair share of the global communications industry. National economies will improve or decline based on acceptance of the implications of the Information Age, fueled by the Telecommunications Act of 1996.

## World's Best Value™

Remember when Bell Atlantic sought to merge with TCI in the mid-1990s in the anticipation of a multimedia revolution? Bell Atlantic followed the failed merger with the creation of a $500 million entertainment and multimedia services company called TeleTV. The new venture was led by Chief Executive Officer Howard Stringer and staffed with experienced Hollywood business people. TeleTV, created on the back of successful video-on-demand trials in Virginia and Italy, was disbanded two years after its creation. Did Bell Atlantic understand the regulatory environment and trends or did they misread the developing global impact of the Internet? A $500 million failed investment may be a small price to pay by an RBOC, but one of the lessons for Bell Atlantic was misunderstanding the regulatory environment and resulting trends.

Howard Stringer is now Chairman and Chief Executive Officer of Sony Corp. of America. Since his arrival at Sony in May, 1997, Sony has invested in CDNow, the top on-line music retailer, digital set-top boxes for television sets and interactive TV initiatives that include interactive versions of *Jeopardy* and *Wheel of Fortune*! Bell Atlantic's TeleTV initiative was either a miscue or a visionary strategy that was ahead of its time.

---

*A **World's Best Value™** company understands*
*the regulatory environment and manages the business*
*based on current and future regulatory trends*

---

36

## Going Global for Competitive Survival

 ### Balance of trade

Countless nations are investing in the Information Age as a matter of national priority. Singapore, for example, has established itself as an Asian center of influence for information technology. The Chinese have always been industrious people and it is not surprising that Chinese make up more than 75 percent of the population in Singapore.

Singapore, with a population of more than one million ethnic Chinese, has established itself as a world-class software development center. The government has taken an active role in this area; witness Singapore Telecom's technology investment fund managed by Vertex that has operations around the world. Singapore Technologies is planning a major push into the Internet arena by building a virtual network in the Asian region.

We should expect growing technology investment funds developing in Europe with centers in Switzerland, England, Netherlands and France. 3i, the leading venture capital company in Europe, is concentrating heavily in the communications area. There is a Silicon Alps in Carinthia, Austria, Silicon Bog in Ireland, Silicon Fen in Cambridge, England and Silicon Glen in Scotland. Northern California is home of Silicon Valley. Rich McGinn, CEO of Lucent Technologies refers to New Jersey as home of the newly phrased *"Photonics Valley."* Many analysts believe that photonics may be one of the next technology growth engines for the communications industry.

37

## World's Best Value™

The Information Age is based on intellectual capital and it is relatively easy to start up *anywhere* in the world, reference the mushrooming software industries in India and Ireland, for example. As the world becomes more *information technology-based*, nations will compete for intellectual capital resources, unlike the natural resources, land and raw materials, that preceded and fueled the agricultural and industrial ages. The new precious capital is human knowledge, and it will determine the balance of power well into the 21st century.

---

*World's Best Value™ nations are competing against other nations for favorable balance of trade and national survival*

---

 ### Policies, politics and people

The United States is providing **World's Best Value™** from a governmental, political, educational and capital generation perspective. While businesses tend to litigate against governmental policies that change the competitive landscape, it must be understood these same policies are meant to stimulate job growth and national economic expansion. Nations must compete on a global basis if they are going to survive. Look at Russia and its decaying agricultural and industrial economy. Among other things, Russia is not able to compete in the supply of agricultural goods to the world because it did not invest in new farming technologies relative to the rest of the world.

Let's examine the North America Free Trade Association and the implications for world trade. In the mid-1990s, Canada, United

## Going Global for Competitive Survival

States and Mexico were in a political uproar regarding free trade between neighboring countries. Economic growth and global survival stimulated the creation of this regional trade policy. What would be the impact on the United States, from an economic perspective, if Canada and Mexico were unable to compete on an international basis? We should look for an Americas free-trading zone that includes North America and Latin America, in the near future, that will be created in response to the historic economic developments in the European Union.

Protectionism in any form is not a sustainable strategy to prevent global competition. The RBOCs in the United States have filed numerous lawsuits regarding the Telecommunications Act of 1996. The RBOC's goal has been to (1) protect local access business, while (2) improving their own ability to offer long distance, and (3) manage the transition of whole network infrastructures to voice, data and video services. The stakes are high as some of the most widely held stocks in the world include Bell South, Bell Atlantic and SBC Communications. The marketplace cannot allow sudden market capitalization reduction due to the governmental policies of unrestricted competition.

---

*Policies, politics and people determine corporate*
*and national conditions that must be addressed by*
***World's Best Value*™** *nations and companies*

---

### World's Best Value™

 ### Winners and losers

There is no guarantee that nations, people or companies will survive in a competitive environment. Just one percent of the people in Asia and less than one percent of Africans have access to the Internet. *Business Week* reported that according to anthropologist and author *Noriyuki Ueda*, Japan's economic slide during the 1990s was the collapse of cultural and spiritual values rooted in deference to authority. The fixation on post World War II growth, has led directly to the bitter aftermath of the bubble economy. The Information Age, by definition, will create an environment of winners and losers. Losing can result in closed businesses, bankruptcy and the downfall of nations. Even though it is not pleasant, losing is a fundamental law of the global competitive environment.

Winning is predicated on skill development, knowledge sharing and teamwork. Sharing knowledge occurs when people are interested in genuinely helping one another develop new capacities for creating learning processes.

Losing is about eroding skills and individualism. If growth is a function of survival, then skills, knowledge, technology, capital and natural resources will be the fuel for growth. The implications for growth are important in a **World's Best Value™** company.

Growth normally means a higher growth rate relative to the market growth rate. How does this happen? Growth happens quite simply at the expense of competitors. In the future, whole industries will shift and merge as companies position for growth and competitive survival. Granted, there will be niche opportunities available, but at some point, the growth machine has to be fed — at the expense of competitors.

---

*A **World's Best Value**™ company knows that sustained growth is required for business survival*

---

 ### The world's largest industry

Let's examine the world's largest industry a bit more closely. Since there are more than six billion people on the planet to feed, why is the world's largest industry not agricultural? Is it the automobile industry, considering the vastness of our worldwide road systems, traffic management, car manufacturing, parts, fuel and other supporting industries? How about the financial industry? Banks, capital markets, lending institutions and investment companies fuel worldwide economic growth. Each of these industries follows the *law of diminishing returns*. While each of the industries noted above are growing, they are growing relative to worldwide population growth.

The Internet is driving a global financial transformation. The World Wide Web is lowering the cost of saving and borrowing, investment capital is increasing as more people have access to financial markets and new financial products and markets are lowering the cost of capital. The capital market is fundamentally changing.

## World's Best Value™

The information industry has become larger than the airline industry and is poised to exceed the publishing industry. The interactive wave is sweeping the United States and the information industry continues to consolidate. MCIWorldCom is merging with Sprint and Bell Atlantic is merging with GTE, following its acquisition of NYNEX.

The world's largest industry is today the automobile industry estimated at $350 billion each year. The auto industry will be surpassed by the information industry early in the next century. Is the automobile industry a growth industry? Why are the market participants merging? Why does the automobile industry have growth and contraction cycles? It is a mature industry that, while growing, is consolidating for efficiency and subsequent growth. Who are the industry leaders and why?

Daimler Benz has acquired Chrysler, which acquired Jeep. Ford Motor Company has acquired Jaguar and Volvo. Volkswagen and BMW fought extremely hard in pursuit of Bentley. In the end, there will be several global automobile competitors that provide **World's Best Value™** products and services to their worldwide customers. This model of consolidation is repeating itself in the financial, energy and pharmaceutical industries. The communications industry is fast following a path of consolidation.

---

*A **World's Best Value™** company in large industries must grow organically as well as by mergers and acquisitions*

---

## Going Global for Competitive Survival

 ## Planes, computers, banks and automobiles

***World's Best Value™*** nations have a mix of industries that must dominate globally in order for companies and nations to prosper. *Gary Hamel*, Visiting Professor of Strategic and International Management at the London Business School, says that competition is more between firms as opposed to competition between nation states.

Let's imagine a doomsday scenario where governments, industries and nations are on the brink of worldwide disaster. The prospect of Armageddon in this imagined scenario could be very real. If we leave out divine intervention, what in the end will prevent worldwide obliteration? What will cause whole nations from crossing the brink of the end of the world, as we know it?

In a melt-down scenario, ultimately, it will come down to individual and national survival instincts. The strong will survive. If a nation were to exploit a technology, such as nuclear weapons, for national expansion interests, the outcome would almost certainly be war or isolation from the rest of the world. Reference Iraq and the Gulf War in the early 1990s. Those countries that have the best people, technology, information, agricultural, manufacturing and financial strength will survive. Planes, computers, banks and automobiles all make a difference, as it relates to global competitive survival.

Global competitive survival has nothing to do with how well you play the game — it has to do with winning. My idealistic side says it does matter how the game is played and there must be a corporate conscience that is linked to the local and worldwide community. Having said that, as a matter of survival, winning is everything! People on the planet should care how their national industries compete on a global basis. Worldwide competition has a lot to do with national safety, growth and survival.

---

*World's Best Value*™ *nations have strong information, financial and manufacturing capabilities that compete and win on a global basis*

---

 *Entertainment is king*

In 1998, Mike Piazza of the New York Mets signed a $91 million, seven-year contract that made him one of the highest paid athletes in professional baseball in the United States. Gene Orza, associate general counsel for the players union predicts that in 100 years, some player will sign a $3 billion contract! Shaquille O'Neal, of the Los Angeles Lakers, signed a $120 million dollar, multi-year contract making him one of the highest paid athletes in all of professional sports.

Sponsors are throwing money at the World Wrestling Federation and NASCAR racing. NASCAR signed a television contract worth more than $400 million putting it in the major league of entertainment. Movies go through no less than 6 levels of distribution including original screening, video tapes, pay per view television, broadcast television, 2nd and 3rd showings before being relegated to reruns or specialty movie channels. *Red Herring Magazine* reports that on-line downloadable CD music will reach revenues of $1.1 billion in 2003. Time Warner bought Turner Broadcasting Corporation for its movies, news and professional sports teams that include the Atlanta Braves. The same holds true for Rupert Murdoch and his purchase of the Los Angeles Dodgers and proposed but ultimately failed purchase of the Manchester United Football club in England.

Cable, satellite and broadcast television have the capacity for hundreds of channels, all requiring content and entertainment. Musicals, dramas, plays, orchestras and much more are in the middle of resurgence throughout the world as economic prosperity enables disposable currency for entertainment. America On Line and Blockbuster have formed a partnership in which Blockbuster will become the number one supplier of America On Line's entertainment channel. Universal Music Group, a division of Seagrams, is going into the on-line music business. Entertainment is one of the fastest growing industries in the world and must compete on a worldwide basis. We will see a continuing trend of consolidation of the entertainment and distribution industries as cornerstones for corporate growth and ultimate survival.

---

*A **World's Best Value**™ company recognizes entertainment as a growth business and has linkages to it that sustain growth and corporate survival*

---

45

### Survival of industries

What is in store for the tobacco industry? What will happen to retail shopping malls? What impact will the Internet have on every business in the world? According to researcher Roper Starch Worldwide Inc., making purchases online was the fastest growing Internet activity in 1999, with 42 percent of Web users shopping online, up from 31 percent in 1998. The Simon Property Group and Prime Realty, two of the largest U.S. retail property owners, have formed new subsidiaries that use Internet technology for their own advantage.

*Fortune magazine* says that the most common failings of chief executive officers are those who (1) were unable to meet or exceed shareowner expectations and (2) did not have a comprehensive Internet strategy in the digital age. *Anticipation* is the underlying attribute of companies and industries that survive and the antithesis of those that do not.

Institutions of higher learning are reaching out to offer courses and degrees for students who never step foot on their campus. Why? In one sense universities and colleges are reaching out to expand their enrollment with minimum capital investment. In another sense they are positioning for the potential wave of the future — borderless learning.

Industrial survival is at risk when men and women in leadership positions fail to see and respond to market and technology trends that will have an impact on the future of their businesses. In the end, survival will boil down to scale and market share or niche participation in a declining market. Typically, when industries survive, it is the production and distribution efficiency that changes. Manually produced goods and services are always at risk given that companies can produce with cheaper labor anywhere in the world. In addition, progress continues in the development of manufacturing and processing technology such as surface mount technology production and robotics.

The rebuilding of Asia is underway. It is too early to tell, for example, what will happen with the Japanese financial and technology industries. But investments in Japan are an early indicator of increasing confidence in the Asian region. Foreign investments in Japan were expected to reach an all-time record of $125 billion in 1999.

---

*World's Best Value™ industries anticipate technology and productivity developments that impact their future*

---

# *World's Best Value*™ **Plan**
## Going Global for Competitive Survival

Objective:     Create a globalization strategy for sustained success and survival

Priorities:

1) Develop a long-term globalization strategy.

2) Create a globalization model to guide actions.

3) Secure board level commitment.

4) Involve leadership in development of strategy.

5) Identify investments that create conditions for success.

6) Analyze competition and create advantage.

7) Learn regulatory environment and maximize resources.

8) Focus on sustained growth for business survival.

9) Balance organic growth with mergers and acquisitions.

10) Anticipate technology and productivity developments.

# Chapter 3

## So You Want To Be A Market Leader

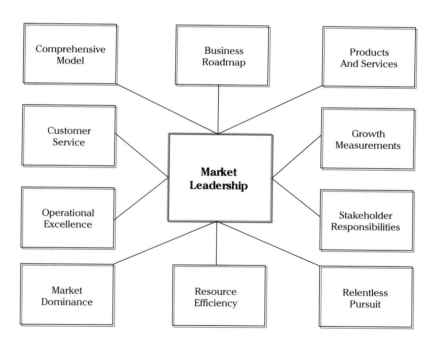

### *So You Want To Be a Market Leader*

 *Market leadership model*

Sustained success in any business requires market leadership in one form or another. Even if your business is the best small business in the least important niche of the largest industry in the world, you need a market leadership model that is adaptable to a changing environment. Marketing strategies must be flexible for companies operating in developing, mature and declining markets.

In the early days of high-speed access to the Internet, low-speed modem technologies were the predominant way to communicate. While new technologies such as ISDN (Integrated Service Digital Network) and subsequent DSL (Digital Subscriber Line) technologies were available in the late 1980s and 1990s respectively, the communications industry was slow to adapt to technological change. It took a long time to translate standards-based networking technology to leading edge digital services for businesses and consumers. The new broadband access lines, such as DSL, are predicted by Ovum, the London-based telecommunications consultancy, to grow to an estimated 27 million lines in 2005 from the more than one million projected for 1999.

Growth potential in mobile telephony is underscored by the new generation of Internet-enabled wireless application protocol technologies being manufactured by Nokia, Ericsson, Alcatel, Motorola and others. Nokia, the world's largest mobile phone producer is developing technology that integrates digital television with the Internet. It has signed a deal with Intel, where the

51

two companies will manufacture set-top boxes for interactive television sets.

The winners in the Information Age revolution will be those companies that adapt to a sea of technology change.

AT&T is betting its strategy on cable investments and is converting their residential cable wires into high-speed digital access lines. Further, AT&T has created a joint venture with BT called Concert, to deliver services to multinational corporations resulting in a combined $10 billion in revenues. The partnership could lead to a merger between the two companies over time. AT&T recently unveiled a wide-ranging new strategy for Latin America by investing in a separately listed company operating in four Latin American countries. The battle lines for Latin America are being drawn to compete against Telefonica of Spain, which has significant interests in the region.

AT&T must be admired as it struggles to transform itself from a monopolistic carrier of local and long distance services to a globally competitive voice, video and data services company. The strategy is risky and the transformation has been slow.

We can learn from the turnaround strategy at Chrysler in the 1980s. Even after the financial bailout by the U.S. government, the company almost went out of business before Lee Iacocca and his team created a marketing differentiation based on engineering leadership. Engineering leadership, mind you, from the same company that developed the Rambler in the 1960s! This marketing leadership model from Chrysler resulted in one of the world's largest mergers and the creation of a globally powerful

Daimler Chrysler company that can compete with any vehicle manufacturer in the world.

So what are the key ingredients to market leadership? Does market leadership need to be complex and require scores of consultants to help map out the success model? Like everything in the business world, market leadership typically boils down to some basic principles. While the devil is in the detail, it is always helpful to know the destination, before one begins a journey. A successful market leadership model needs to focus on differentiated products and services, customer service, operational excellence and new market creation and dominance.

---

*A **World's Best Value**™ company has a comprehensive marketing leadership model that provides a roadmap for differentiation and success*

---

 ### Differentiated products and services

Every company has products and services. So why are some companies more successful than others? How is success measured? Is it market share or volume growth on a quarter-by-quarter basis? Scotty's, a home improvement company based in Florida, thought it had the model right. Although Scotty's is located in one of the fastest growing regions of the country, it did not have the vision or resources to expand nationwide and as a result has been relegated to a second-tier player in the fast growing home-improvement supplies market. Did somebody say Home Depot?

## *World's Best Value™*

It really is not enough to have the best products or the best services. The consumers must *perceive* products and services to be the best. The perception of best products, services or companies is almost always reinforced by brand awareness. Ultimately, products and services in every market segment will have competition and brand is a key differentiator.

Is it a coincidence that companies with powerful product and service brands tend to dominate more than 80 percent of large markets? In the automotive industry it is Ford, Daimler Chrysler, General Motors, Volkswagen and Toyota. In the consumer electronics industry it is Philips, Panasonic and Sony. In the fast-food industry it is McDonald's, Burger King, PepsiCo (KFC, Taco Bell) Subway and Wendy's. So the next time you are sitting in a product management meeting and a new product idea is discussed, ask a simple question, *"how will we differentiate this product and service from every other product and service in the marketplace?"*

---

*Differentiated products and services are an*
*essential part of a market leadership model*

---

 ***Outstanding customer service***

How easy is it to fix product problems when they occur? Recently, I spoke by phone to a customer service representative for my wireless service provider who actually introduced herself by name. She thanked me for using her company's service and let me know that if there was a problem in the future, to feel free to contact her directly. I was amazed at the professional courtesy and personal attention to detail!

I called United Airlines in the United States recently to make a reservation from Tampa to Cincinnati. I thought it would be a pretty simple exercise. I was wrong! I had to patiently work my way though five levels of automated telephone message screening to make sure the call went to the right attendant. United is a fine airline, but my experience here was not up to my expectations of excellent customer service. No doubt it is more efficient for the airline, but was frustrating for me, the consumer.

Compare a recent experience, when my wife Jill and I flew between London, England and Glasgow, Scotland. We boarded a British Airways flight and had no less than five attendants welcome us on board and wished us a good day. Given that we were flying coach, it was a quality experience that I would have normally experienced only in first class!

How should a business account for customer service? Is it an expense item or a profit center? Is it a necessary cost of doing business or a marketing tool to build brand loyalty and product usage? Is it a place for the very best people or a rotational assignment for mediocre employees?

World-class customer service can be either a cost or profit center depending on the company and the industry. Whether a cost or profit center, world-class customer service is consistently staffed with the best and the brightest people in companies that want to provide **World's Best Value™** products and services. The people are almost always well educated about the company's products and services and are trained in interpersonal communications and customer satisfaction. Outstanding customer service is *always* an essential ingredient in any market leadership model. The old adage still applies, *"it is relatively easy to gain new customers, and just as easy to loose them with poor customer service."*

---

*Outstanding customer service is an essential*
*part of market leadership models*

---

 ### Operational excellence

It is not enough to provide just quality goods and services in a global economy. Quality must extend beyond the manufacturing environment. It must reach the boardroom and every operational process in between. If we stop and think for a minute, market leadership must synthesize every business process that occurs in the company. It does no good to create brand and product differentiation if poor quality billing practices cost customers money.

In *World's Best Value*™ companies, operational excellence is based on zero-tolerance for anything that increases the cost of operations and diminishes customer satisfaction. Is *Quality Job 1* at Ford Motor Company or is it just a jingle? How did Saturn find its niche in a crowded automobile industry? Why was there room for yet another car company in the United States in the 1980s? The business foundation of Saturn is to put the customer first in conjunction with operational excellence.

### *So You Want To Be a Market Leader*

Have you heard of Hamburger University at McDonald's? McDonald's is in the mass-market, fast food business and knows that operational excellence is the difference between success and failure as well as profit and loss.

Any transaction-based business demands operational excellence. Why are there so many mergers and acquisitions in the financial services, communications, retailing and automotive industries? It starts with scalability and growth; and ends with operational excellence. Large numbers of business transactions require operational excellence. The opposite is true for high cost, low transaction businesses. We can be sure that Rolex, a worldwide leader in selling high-quality jewelry and timepieces, is concerned about operational excellence.

---

*A **World's Best Value**™ company recognizes operational excellence as a key ingredient for sustained market leadership*

---

 ### *Create and dominate new markets*

If growth is the key to business survival, then creation and dominance of new markets is the key to market leadership. It is possible to be a market follower, but only those global corporations with considerable brand, distribution channels and price advantage are able to successfully execute a market-follower model. New market creation is a constant desire to expand and grow business opportunities. Dominance in any chosen market has become the widely-accepted philosophy of sustained market leadership. General Electric and Microsoft know something about market dominance and they reward their shareowners every day, every month, every quarter and every year with their financial performance and stock appreciation. When Jack Welch took over in 1981, General Electric sales increased from $27 billion to $100 billion in 1998, and profits from $1.6 billion to $9.2 billion in the same timeframe.

Since when did consumers have a bagel once, twice or every day during the week? It began when Einstein Bagels decided to institutionalize the mass-market for bagels. When did it become essential to have specialty coffee in every airport in just about every corner of the world? It began when Starbucks decided it should be so. How about affordable car leasing for everyone? It began when the car companies decided to take the financial risks away from consumers and remove financial impediments by creating leasing for new car purchases every few years.

New markets do not just happen they are created. *The winners do not just participate they dominate.* Find companies with a winning philosophy and you will find **World's Best Value™**.

---

*A **World's Best Value™** company consistently creates new markets for business growth and dominates for sustained financial performance*

---

## So You Want To Be a Market Leader

 ### Resources make the difference

Watch out for any market leadership model that does not assign the necessary resources for success. Many employees have been part of teams that has the will, but falls short on the way. A team's effort to create growth and market leadership is not always matched by the efficient application of resources required to generate success.

The day Bill Gates decided to dominate the software that controls access of a personal computer to the Internet, was the day he applied several hundred software engineers to work on the problem. How many times have we seen pioneers in any industry, fall short of the financial resources necessary to flourish and grow their business? Venture capital funding in the second quarter of 1999 was at $7.6 billion with more than half of the funds going to Internet start-ups. God bless venture capitalists like Harry Fitzgibbons, Managing Director of Top Technology, the venture capital industry, and all of the risk takers in the world who are betting on new digital networking technologies and multimedia service offerings. Without the application of their financial resources, the Information Age would take longer to develop.

---

*A **World's Best Value**™ company knows how to efficiently apply human and capital resources to business opportunities*

---

59

### Relentless pursuit

The relentless pursuit of market leadership is another key to sustained success. Human nature and business processes are by definition fallible. There will always be problems to face and obstacles to overcome. The difference is relentless pursuit. It seems to me that Lexus has got it right in branding *"The Relentless Pursuit of Perfection."* How can anyone argue with that?

Perseverance, dedication, consistency and stick-to-itiveness describe what it takes to be successful. The United States became the leading nuclear power in the world when it relentlessly pursued the creation of a weapon of mass destruction that would end WWII. Putting a man on the moon only happened when hundreds of thousands of men and women relentlessly pursued the dream of space travel.

---

*A **World's Best Value™** company is committed
to the relentless pursuit of market leadership*

---

 ### Anticipate everything

Why settle for anything other than your goals? In a world-class marketing leadership model, you can and should anticipate everything. *Peter Senge's* groundbreaking work on systems thinking in *The Fifth Discipline* is a good place to understand the necessary system skills that enable each of us to anticipate the unexpected. Why should market leadership be any different than a doctor diagnosing a patient? It's fine to specialize but only in the context of understanding the entire system.

### So You Want To Be a Market Leader

It is not acceptable in a market leadership model to be blind-sided by competition or your customers. Businesses should know their competitor's plans and activities at least as well as their own if they are to be marketing leaders. Granted, it is easier to ignore or have an incomplete understanding of your competition. It is easier to focus only on your own business.

In anticipation of competition in the Information Age, Nortel Networks is dramatically changing from a stodgy telecommunications equipment supplier to a nimble Silicon Valley entrepreneurial-like company. For example, it is putting more emphasis on selling products online. *Business Week* reported that leading the charge is an ex-ski instructor from Bay Networks who is heading a 40-member team in Santa Clara to overhaul Nortel's Web site. When a skier takes-off down the mountain, it would be dangerous to think that he or she does not know the course or is unaware of competitive threats to success. Such actions, literally, would be a recipe for disaster.

---

*A **World's Best Value™** company anticipates everything related to competitive threats*

---

 ### In pursuit of the leader

Competition is healthy. Or at least the market winners say so. It sure does not feel like winning when your business division or company goes out of business. It does not feel like winning when your business has to downsize. Let's look at it another way. If your business pursues the leader, emulates the leader, runs faster, harder and smarter than the leader, you will eventually be a market leader.

Competitive sport is a great learning environment for business. Championship dreams become a reality when ownership, management, coaches and players come together. Pursuit of leadership creates a healthy environment for success and achievement.

One thing missing in business is the art of *mentoring*. Mentors take the time to help high-potential people and businesses develop their full potential. Mentors know that businesses should emulate competitors and market leaders. The key is to take what works! Everyone, including market leaders have bad habits. Even market leaders are not perfect. However, they do more right than wrong. General Electric is a model for corporate efficiency. It has it's growth engine firing on all cylinders and GE customers, employees and investors love it. The Hay Consultancy Group conducted a survey and ranks General Electric as the most admired company in the United States. How many businesses in any industry have taken the time to actually study how GE operates?

---

A *World's Best Value*™ company emulates
successful market leaders

---

 **Why be bigger?**

In many respects, growth is a lot easier to accomplish than operational efficiency. So why be bigger? Most companies measure success by year over year revenue growth. It is an expression, typically, of market share gained. It is not a bad way of looking at your business as long as profitability and cash flow are given due consideration. No business in the world can operate without cash. So is bigger, better?

Being big must be measured in some sort of context. Is the business growing in a growing market? Is it declining in a declining market? Is it staying the same in a declining market? Being a big business can only be measured in context of what is happening in the marketplace. It is like anything else. Size has to be measured in relationship to the industry and competition. The next time a business associate asks if you are part of a big business, ask the following question in return, *"compared to what?"*

---

*A **World's Best Value**™ company measures*
*growth and size of it's business in context*
*of the industry and marketplace*

---

 ### It's OK to be number one

The best advice a successful person ever gave me was to not be afraid of success! There comes a time in everyone's life where a person reaches the brink of being as good as they can be, and they become afraid of taking the next step. A world-class company that consistently provides value to customers, shareowners and employees understands *investments* in people are required to be number one.

When was the last time your company invested in you? Is your business taking the time to *nurture* your development? Is your company investing in the *communities* in which it operates? Does your company have the financial resources to continue to be first? Typically, sustained industry leadership requires mergers and acquisitions in order to acquire new technologies, skill sets and complimentary businesses that increase shareowner value.

Organic growth typically takes too long and is too hard to accomplish. As good as Wal-Mart knows, for example, that it will need to grow its business operations outside of the United States in order to remain a market leader.

If you ask any successful person or sports figure what is next thought they have after they win a championship or achieve their goals, the answer is almost always to win another championship or remain on top. It is human nature to want to leave a legacy and be judged against past and future greatness and success.

---

*A **World's Best Value**™ company treasures the opportunity to be first and is unafraid of success*

---

 ## Responsibilities of a market leader

The price of being number one is accepting the *responsibilities of leadership*. It is disappointing when a recognized sports figure sheds any responsibility for giving back to the fans and the community. Likewise, a market leader must acknowledge their impact on others.

Let's start with *responsibilities to customers*. Market leadership is providing customers with the best value products and services or directing them to companies that can fulfill their needs. Market leadership is innovating and listening to your customer requirements.

What are *the responsibilities to shareowners*? Quite simply, it is to provide the best return on your shareowners investment relative to any other competitor in your industry sector and better than any company in any market. Amazon.com chief executive, Jeffrey Bezos, for instance, is ambitiously transforming his company to an on-line e-commerce portal for everything.

The growth strategy for his shareowners is his new zShops initiative that is targeting small merchants and individuals to sell their goods to the more than 12 million Amazon.com customers. Men and women invest money with expectations of growth, corporate stewardship and significant return. Oh, by the way, investors have choices and they are rightfully demanding.

Market leaders are *responsible to their employees* to provide an environment for learning and productive work. Training, education, performance feedback and challenging work assignments are characteristics of a learning environment.

Finally, market leaders are *responsible to the communities* they operate in. The very same people that consume products and services are part of a community that creates an environment for business success. It is a partnership.

---

*A **World's Best Value**™ company is responsible to shareowners, customers, employees and communities*

---

# *World's Best Value*™ **Plan**
## So You Want To Be a Market Leader

Objective: Determine the requirements for market leadership.

Priorities:

1) Create a comprehensive market leadership model.

2) Develop roadmap for differentiation and success.

3) Focus on differentiated products and services.

4) Create a world-class customer service capability.

5) Implement a culture of operational excellence.

6) Create and dominate markets for sustained success.

7) Efficiently apply human and capital resources.

8) Relentlessly pursue market leadership.

9) Measure growth in context of industry and market.

10) Be responsible to stakeholders.

# Chapter 4

## Customer Satisfaction is Everything

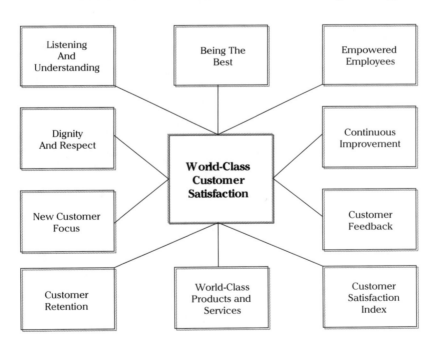

## Customer Satisfaction is Everything

 ### Listen, understand and deliver

In **World's Best Value™** companies, *"customer satisfaction is not the only thing, it is everything!"* Early in their corporate development, **World's Best Value™** companies realized that a very large percentage of their business comes from current or existing customers. The airlines know it. The banks know it. The communications service providers know it. If everyone knows it, why is is it so hard to implement and sustain?

Gary Seamans, former Chairman of Westell Technologies, a networking company located in Aurora, Illinois, implemented a simple yet powerful business philosophy that said; *we listen — we understand — we deliver*. It became the mantra for all employees to rally around a way of doing business. The foundation was around customer satisfaction.

We have all been in conversations with people who dominate a discussion. These people were very poor listeners and constantly thinking about their next response as opposed to hearing what you had to say. I know I've been in business meetings with business associates were so busy selling what they had, they forgot to listen to what their customer wanted.

*Listening* is a lost art. The art of listening is based on highly refined communications skills and many people do not take the time to ask questions for understanding before formulating their own response. Poor communications, which includes the inability to listen, is often cited as a key reason for business inefficiency.

The continuum next considers *understanding*. How can understanding really take place without first listening? Understanding is asking questions. It is about probing for clarification. It is actively engaging in what we know and do not know, and being open to learning. If you want to learn about the French culture, don't eat at Burger King in Paris! Understanding is about being open to new ideas and comfortable with different points of view. I like to reflect on business decisions and ask the question, *"What did we learn from this"*?

*Delivering* is the final step in the continuum after learning and understanding. Delivering outcomes and results will create customer satisfaction. Don't you thoroughly enjoy talking to a customer service representative who is empowered to help you solve problems? I often say that the two finest words in the English language are *no problem*! You see, no problem, means that the customer service representative listened to my issues, understood their value to me as a customer, and was prepared to deliver a result to my complete satisfaction.

---

*A **World's Best Value™** company listens,*
*understands and delivers solutions to a*
*customer's complete and total satisfaction*

---

 ### Focus on being the best

Customer satisfaction does not happen by accident. When the Universal Card division of AT&T in the early 1990s became an overnight sensation in the crowded credit card industry, it focused on being the best in the industry. Universal Card interest rates were less than half the industry standard. A significant effort was put into employee training and information systems. AT&T Universal Card took competitive pricing and world-class customer satisfaction to new levels. In its first several months of operations, Universal Card had signed up one million new customers and created a sea-change trend towards competitive pricing in the personal finance industry.

When was the last time you heard an employee say, *"I think I'll do just average work today?"* Life in general, and business in particular, is fleeting in time. Why not be the best? I returned a modem to CompUSA the other day without a receipt. I was frustrated that my personal computer could not access the Internet. When the modem was returned, the main focus of the customer service representative was how he could help me solve my problem. Minutes later, I had a new modem with minimum delay and without further frustration.

Let me clarify that being the best in customer satisfaction, is relative to the industry, not the best that you can be. Individual greatness cannot overcome poor business practices. Individual greatness can go a long way, but is eventually unsustainable. Focus on being the best is about people, processes, productivity tools and commitment to customer satisfaction.

---

*A **World's Best Value**™ company focuses on being the best at providing world-class customer service*

---

## World's Best Value™

 *How easy are you to do business with?*

The last thing customers with a problem want to know is why a business cannot solve a problem. While people make the customer satisfaction experience painful or pleasant; business practices, processes and productivity tools enable complete customer satisfaction. In a geographically dispersed business, information is king. Employees must have on-line access to relevant information they need to solve a customer's problem.

I once traveled on TWA from Winnipeg, Canada to Tampa, Florida and stopped at Minneapolis, Minnesota in transit. As a multi-million mile flyer on American Airlines, I have become accustomed to receiving outstanding customer service. Because of my long-time patronage and frequent flying history, American consistently treats me like a very special customer. They speak to me with respect and are always helpful. In my Minneapolis experience with TWA, it was clear that I was being treated like the man in the moon! The computers were down, the supervisor was unavailable to assist, the attendants were clearly not empowered to solve my problem and guess what? It was a travel disaster for me. I have hesitated flying on TWA since, but take note that TWA was recognized recently as number one in JD Power customer satisfaction for short-haul flights, so there must be hope.

Granted, computers go down. But what were the back-up plans and what were the contingencies to deal with a problem such as mine? Supervisors sometimes have other priorities. No doubt this was true in my situation. But what was the plan to help

72

live paying customers in this kind of situation? And finally, why can't educated men and women be held accountable for their actions and be responsible to solve their customer's problems? Customers like to work with people and companies that are easy to do business with. The Internet explosion will no doubt create challenges and opportunities for improved customer satisfaction and ease of doing business.

---

*A **World's Best Value™** company is easy to do business with and empowers people to solve customer problems*

---

 ### *Please treat me like a customer*

In the final analysis, companies who lose sight of their customers either loose market share or go out of business. Remember when K-Mart and J.C. Penney dominated the retail industry? Eastern Airlines and Pan Am used to dominate international travel to Asia, Europe, Latin America and beyond. Somewhere along the line, these companies incurred significant financial difficulties and as a result lost sight of their employees and customers. In the airline industry, customers had a choice. Pan Am and Eastern customers left the airlines in droves.

Flying is not easy for most people. In order to provide outstanding customer service, **World's Best Value™** companies treat their employees with dignity and respect and expect the same in return from customers.

The automobile industry has historically been notorious for providing terrible customer service. Lexus built its business around excellent customer service and Ford, GM, Daimler-Chrysler and others are running hard to catch up. When was the last time you got outstanding customer service from your cable operator or for that matter your local telephone service provider?

Sir Ian Vallance, Chairman of British Telecommunications PLC ("BT") said in a *Wall Street Journal* interview, *"The major challenges for the communications industry are not primarily technological. The really successful communications companies will be those that build up the best relationships with their customers and help them make the most of the enormous opportunities that the digital world presents."*

The digital revolution is well underway and the telecommunications act of 1996 in the United States has spurred competition resulting in a feeding frenzy by communications service providers for new customers. AT&T's purchase of TCI and MediaOne is an all out assault for local access to customers. Given AT&T's relatively good track record in providing customer service, there may be hope after all for the cable operators. What we once knew as a broadcast cable TV system will be upgraded to provide voice, video and data over coaxial cable and twisted copper wire. This scenario is being replicated in the rest of North America, Europe, Asia and Latin America. *World's Best Value™* companies must never lose sight it is easier to gain new customers than it is to keep them.

---

*A **World's Best Value™** company treats
customers with dignity and respect*

---

### Customer Satisfaction is Everything

 *While you were away*

There are literally millions of businesses around the world, many of which are competing for the same customer. *Running scared* and being paranoid are not overstatements as it relates to getting and keeping your best customers. Given the relative inefficiency of many companies and economies around the world, many believe the sum total of each business plan related to a particular market, is over-subscribed.

Let's examine new technology companies, especially in start-up markets. Each has its own view of the opportunity and resources required to exploit the business. The problem is that each 15 percent market share assumption for the 20 companies pursuing the market, adds up to 300 percent market share! If the market is interesting, like the communications marketplace, and holds promise for growth and expansion, the inevitable result is reduction in prices, industry consolidation and resulting business failures.

Customer satisfaction can be impacted when we are not attending to our customers. While business leaders and their employees are focusing on other customers and other business opportunities, a competitor across the street, around the block, across town, on the other side of the country or world, is probably planning ways to reach your customers.

On-line commerce is a threat to traditional customer relationships and exposes the issue of customer focus and attention. CarDirect.com, for example, is an on-line company that lets customers research, configure, purchase, finance, insure and deliver a car to their home or residence. This new transaction-configuration business is supported by a $10 million investment from MSD Capital, founded by Michael Dell, Chairman of Dell Computer. CarDirect.com is utilizing e-commerce to earn market share at the expense of competitors who are still using traditional methods of distribution.

---

*A **World's Best Value**™ company constantly focuses on gaining and keeping customers in order to mitigate worldwide competitive threats*

---

 ### All I want is World's Best Value™

Customers are pretty simple. They want a product or service that works the first time, every time. They want good quality at an affordable price and they want to work with a company that stands behind its products and services and provides world-class customer service. If we think about it, they are not asking for much.

Wal-Mart is a good example of getting it right with customers. They see a need unfulfilled in the marketplace and are relentlessly working to meet or exceed customer expectations. Have you been in a Wal-Mart lately? The experience transcends socio-economic considerations. It is a low-cost, quality experience.

We can sometimes forget that people buy from people. People in responsible positions, such as purchasing, are motivated to get the highest-quality lowest-cost products for their manufacturing process or customers. The purchase of sub-standard products and services can have a very negative consequence for continuing employment and business profitability!

---

*Customers want **World's Best Value**™
products and services from their suppliers*

---

 **Measure, improve and measure again**

What is world-class customer satisfaction? How would a business know if it is world-class? Once world-class customer satisfaction is achieved, what is next? There are probably more questions than answers related to the measurement of customer satisfaction. The key is to create a measurement system, improve on it and measure again. The process never ends because the customer requirements keep changing. Customer satisfaction is a challenging and exciting business function that must be measured and constantly improved.

My experience in dealing with companies such as Motorola, 3M, British Telecom, AT&T, Lucent Technologies, Cisco and Nippon Electric Corporation is they all have different methods of measuring customer satisfaction. The common thread is they each HAVE a measurement system.

The best companies look at a number of aspects to measure customer satisfaction. Intuitively, this makes sense so customer satisfaction like everything else can be put in some sort of measurable context.

### *World's Best Value*™

A *customer satisfaction index composite* is a very good way to get started. It can take the emotion out of any one good or bad measurement and blend those things that your business and customers think is important. A customer satisfaction index that I favor would include the following measurements:

Customer Satisfaction Index

| | Current Ranking | Highest Score |
|---|---|---|
| • On time delivery as measured by request date | .8 | 1.0 |
| • Percentage of sales to existing customers | .6 | 1.0 |
| • Defects per million for units of production | .9 | 1.0 |
| • Returned goods as a percentage of total shipments | .8 | 1.0 |
| • Cost of sales decrease over time | .7 | 1.0 |
| • Operating expenses decrease over time | .9 | 1.0 |
| | 4.7 | 6.0 |

For the sake of argument, let's say the composite index above is the sum total of 4.7 on a scale of six being the highest ranking. Improvements or setbacks in any of the areas will move the index each time period and provide a useful way of measuring customer satisfaction. The key is to get started, measure, improve and measure again. Your customers will love the fact that you care enough about them. Be prepared for customers to provide input on what they think is important!

---

*Companies that provide **World's Best Value™**
continuously measure and improve customer satisfaction*

---

 **What your customers don't tell you is a problem**

The Japanese culture is right to demand courteous behavior in business. The Japanese can be very polite and accommodating even in disagreement. Western businesses can find it difficult to work with these characteristics of the Japanese culture. Despite language barriers, western business people often respect the business acumen of their Japanese counterparts.

Western business people can also struggle with the Japanese not explicitly disagreeing with points of view. The Japanese will often nod their heads in seeming *approval* at business meetings. In fact, however, the Japanese are only *acknowledging* that they understand!

The same can be true with your customers. They can grow so tired and disrespectful of your company's product and services that they nod their heads, knowing full well that they have written your company off as a long-term supplier. You would much rather know the problems and issues with customers then to receive little or no feedback. Think of your customer as you would any other valued relationship and it is better to deal with the issues, for better or worse. When customers stop talking, it is time to worry on a world-class basis!

---

A **World's Best Value™** *company seeks
customer views on needs for improvement*

---

# *World's Best Value*™ **Plan**
## Customer Satisfaction is Everything

Objective: Build a world-class customer satisfaction culture.

Priorities:

1) Deliver solutions based on listening and understanding.

2) Focus on being the best.

3) Empower employees to solve customer problems.

4) Treat customers with dignity and respect.

5) Focus on gaining and keeping customers.

6) Mitigate competitive threats with customer retention.

7) Provide world-class products and services.

8) Develop customer satisfaction index for measurement.

9) Continuously improve measurement systems.

10) Constantly seek customer feedback for improvement.

# Chapter 5

## Do We Really Hear Our Customers?

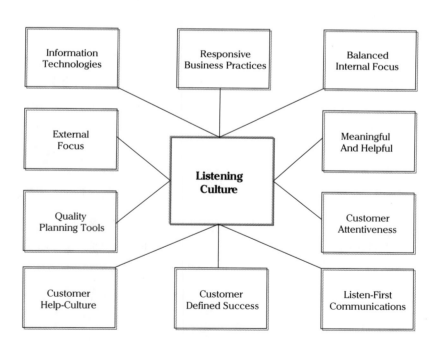

Information Technologies

Responsive Business Practices

Balanced Internal Focus

External Focus

Meaningful And Helpful

**Listening Culture**

Quality Planning Tools

Customer Attentiveness

Customer Help-Culture

Customer Defined Success

Listen-First Communications

### Do We Really Hear Our Customers?

 *Customer focus vs. internal focus*

The challenge for all businesses is to keep the right balance between customer focus and internal processes. Striking the balance is easier said than done. Many employees in even the best companies in the world do not have direct customer interaction and therefore lack full customer perspective. Unfortunately, many jobs do not require employees to interact with external customers nor do the companies train or rotate assignments to ensure the balance is well understood.

On the other hand, we have all seen companies that are so intently focused on serving external customers; they overlook internal processes that enable intensive customer focus to be replicated. Start-up companies, in particular, can easily fall into this trap. While seeking new customers, start-ups do not always put the right emphasis on quality procedures and business processes. In this situation, human energy is focused on external customer demands as opposed to creating repeatable business processes. Customer satisfaction will decline in an environment of unbalanced external focus.

Disney, Hewlett Packard and Federal Express have excellent customer focus. It is well documented that each company has invested heavily in the underlying information technology and business practices that enable their employees to provide the right level of customer focus. I have yet to hear of a child, young person or adult who has been to Disney World complain about the quality of their experience (other than perhaps the long lines!).

---

*A **World's Best Value™** company invests in business practices and information technologies that enable the right balance between customer focus and internal focus*

---

 ### Products that reflect customer's needs

One of the saddest and most frustrating business experiences for a company is when new products are developed without consideration of customer needs. Believe it or not, it happens in all industries and is especially true in companies that are heavily dependent on new technologies. Rapid changes in technology can have a dramatic negative impact on new product introduction, especially in new emerging market segments.

What are the customer's needs? Have you ever been in a situation where ten people were asked about customer requirements and there were ten different answers and perspectives? There is always healthy contention between sales, marketing and engineering on this question as well. The best way to reach consensus is to apply the science of prioritizing product features and customer needs. In fact, customer needs, can often be the result of a technology push creating the need. For example, in the communications industry, the Internet is creating huge demand for higher speed access for communications with voice, video and data services.

Hewlett Packard is using the Internet to remake itself from a computer manufacturer to an electronic services company. It plans to charge its customers a percentage of transaction revenues. Ann Livermore, CEO of HP's $14 billion Enterprise Com-

84

## *Do We Really Hear Our Customers?*

puting Solutions said in a *Business Week* interview that she anticipates 80 percent of the division's future revenues could come from electronic services.

Let's look at an example of designing the next generation sports car. How important is speed, aerodynamic design, passenger space, quality road tires, weight of the car versus thousands of other details that make up the next generation sports car? A methodical, well thought through, disciplined approach to this kind of decision-making will help prioritize product features in the context of customer needs.

Products that reflect customers' needs
Prioritization Matrix – "World-Car" Platform
1 – Low / 5 – High

| Feature | U.S. | Japan | Europe | Asia | Total |
|---|---|---|---|---|---|
| Range of color selection | 4 | 3 | 4 | 2 | 13 |
| Lightweight | 2 | 4 | 5 | 3 | 14 |
| Ample passenger space | 3 | 2 | 2 | 4 | 11 |
| Aerodynamic design | 4 | 3 | 4 | 2 | 13 |
| Alloy wheel covers | 2 | 3 | 4 | 3 | 12 |
| Leather interior | 5 | 3 | 5 | 3 | 16 |
| Automatic transmission | 4 | 3 | 2 | 2 | 11 |
| Brand name tires | 3 | 4 | 3 | 3 | 13 |

This simplified example enables a group of people from different countries and regions of the world to quantify what they

85

believe are the most important attributes of a world-car platform. It can be further extended to mathematically weight the importance of each country or region on the total. It is a powerful tool to help quantify opinions and prioritize decisions. The real fun and usefulness is in the discussion that goes along with reaching consensus on the various attributes! In this example, leather interior (16) and a lightweight vehicle (14) were considered the most important features of a global automobile platform and ample passenger space (11) and automatic transmission (11) were considered the least important.

---

*A **World's Best Value**™ company uses quality tools to help design products that meet customer needs*

---

 ### *Helping your customer be successful*

When was the last time a business looked at customers in a way that considered how to make the customer successful? Helping customers be successful is a powerful thought that puts business on the side of customers. For example, when customers share their business case information, it removes emotion and uncertainty about "fair" pricing from customers perspectives. This practice puts two formidable groups, the supplier and customer, on the same side of solving the problem.

British Telecom is considered one of the leading communications service providers in a marketplace, the United Kingdom, is widely considered the second most competitive communications market outside of the United States. BT made an announcement in the summer of 1999 to wire nearly 6 million homes to provide high-speed access to the Internet using its embedded copper infrastructure.

Of course, the decision by BT was more than 5 years in planning. What is so exciting about the announcement is BT's novel approach to partnering with key networking equipment suppliers. BT shared their business case information and provided an opportunity for financial risk and gain sharing. As it turns out Fujitsu and Alcatel were the chosen suppliers in a competitive bid process. No doubt each supplier wakes up every day worrying about how to make BT successful. This model is often used in new infrastructure build scenarios in high technology as well as commercial building projects.

SBC Communications has a similar partnering model with Alcatel, IBM and others. SBC Communications is transforming its local telephone access network to a high-speed digital network capable of delivering new Internet and multimedia services. Customer demands and enormous growth opportunities dictate partnering solutions from best of breed companies who can work together and provide end-to-end solutions. Partnering is a way of life in the communications industry.

Sun Microsystems and Sony, for example, are combining their efforts to create Internet devices for home networking, set top box and digital videodisk applications. Microsoft is partnering with Radio Shack to reach Internet customers in Radio Shack retail outlets across the United States.

## World's Best Value™

*Making customers successful* is an advanced level of thinking that separates world-class companies from the rest. Customer-success thinking puts business in a stewardship state of mind making customer success the dominant thought process. Try it; your customers will love it!

---

*A **World's Best Value™** company has a strong culture to help customers be successful*

---

 ### Who defines success?

Who is responsible for defining success in a business transaction? Is it the company we own or work for? Is it your immediate manager? Is it the shareowners? Classic financial management says success is typically measured in revenues and profits. I don't think customers define success in those same terms.

Customers simply define success based on their complete satisfaction with consumption of a product or service.

Revenues, profits and growth are all by-products of customer satisfaction. In its simplest form, if customers are not satisfied consuming your product and service, you will not have long-term customers. So the next time you discuss business success, bring the customers' perspective into the debate. I promise it will be a lively and enlightening discussion.

---

*Customers define success in*
***World's Best Value™** companies*

---

## Do We Really Hear Our Customers?

 ### *So much to say, does anyone care?*

How many times have you seen a business colleague busily prepare for an important meeting and get so caught up in preparation, that he or she forgets the purpose of the meeting? We see it all the time. The sounds of one's own voice can be alluring. The sound of one's voice can create a trance where every sense of business discipline gets thrown out the window.

The most visible example can almost always be seen at an awards banquet. How many times have we seen an Oscar award-winner ramble for so long, thanking so many people that the world-wide audience loses interest? What are the Oscar *ramblers* thinking? It happens all the time.

It is common in technology businesses to see bright engineering, sales and marketing people in deep product and technology discussions. But is there real communication going on in those deep conversations? Or is it one-way communications? Based on the popularity of the technically irreverent *Dilbert* cartoon and books, many do believe there is a communications gap between technical and non-technical business functions. I know I have often found myself in conversations where I ask someone for the time, and they tell me how to build a watch! Do not do that with your customers!

---

*World's Best Value™ people have a lot to say and they make sure communications are meaningful and helpful*

---

# *World's Best Value*™ **Plan**
## Do We Really Hear Our Customers?

Objective:  Develop a listening culture.

Priorities:

1) Invest in information technologies.

2) Create customer responsive business practices.

3) Balance internal focus to better serve customers.

4) Focus externally to better hear customer requirements.

5) Use quality tools for customer-driven products.

6) Create a culture that helps customers be successful.

7) Recognize customers define success for companies.

8) Develop a listen-first communications style.

9) Ensure communications are meaningful and helpful.

10) Continuously measure customer attentiveness.

# Chapter 6

## Perception is Reality

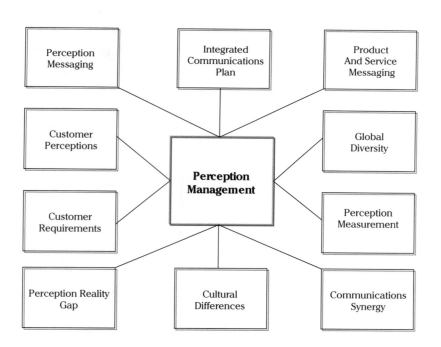

### Perception is Reality

 ### Paradigms tell stories

Billions of dollars are invested each year in start-up companies that promise to be the "next Microsoft" or the "next Yahoo". A robust world economy has made traditional financial institutions, and wealthy individuals for that matter, look for places to put their cash and willing to take risks! The world has become a global media machine. Press announcements, trade press, mainstream papers and magazines such as *The Wall Street Journal* and *Time* forge reality.

There is so much information and misinformation in the marketplace that the head of marketing communications can be as important as the head of engineering in the *value creation process*. Every company is trying to get their *message* out and compete with other messages in the marketplace. Everyone has his or her own perspective or *paradigm* which is really the way one sees things. It is important, however, to understand the paradigm of your customers and the investing public so they will perceive your messaging in the way intended.

On November 1, 1999, Ford ran a global TV *roadblock* that was intended to reach a global audience of millions with the goal to generate warm and fuzzy feelings about Ford as a world-leading company for auto products and services. The two-minute broadcast ran in New Zealand on that date and worked its way around the world. The commercial was intended to help welcome the millennium and celebrate the diversity of Ford's customers. Ford addressed its customers paradigm by investing $10 million of commercial time with dozens of national and pan-regional networks that includes 40 broadcast and cable channels in the United States alone!

I have always been concerned about the media-hype machine until I understood how it works. Garrick Case, president at PR Plus International, a public relations and advertising agency located in Florida, is quick to point out there are hundreds of messages crossing a news editors desk each day. A company's messaging has to be new, different and ideally an industry first. Most importantly it must be perceived as newsworthy. There is still media-hype in the marketplace, but ultimately, branding boils down to creating a perception of differentiated companies, products and services as seen by customers, employees, investors and the public at large.

---

*Perception is an important factor when developing market messages for customers, investors, employees and the public*

---

 ### What you see is not what your customers get

How many times have we seen companies believe so strongly in their own communications, they are oblivious to reality? I have found this to be true with product announcements. A product manager, for instance, can be so close to the development of a product, he or she fails to communicate customer benefits resulting from use of the product.

Let's look at corporate communications in an environment of safety concerns and consumer backlash. In the 1980s, Johnson and Johnson faced a product safety scare when Tylenol products were found in several U.S. locations to have traces of arsenic. While Johnson and Johnson was arguably blameless, they decided to immediately remove all Tylenol pain reliever products from the store shelves across the United States. Johnson and Johnson decided to move quickly and deal with customer confidence issues, in an environment of product tampering. Consumer confidence in Johnson and Johnson actually increased after the product scare and the Tylenol brand remains one of the strongest in the industry.

Another example is how Coca-Cola responded to product tampering in Europe during 1999. Under similar circumstances to Johnson and Johnson, Coca-Cola did not take immediate aggressive actions to remove contaminated Coca-Cola product from store shelves in Belgium and elsewhere. European Union government and customer backlash against Coca-Cola was very negative because of the way Coca-Cola dealt with this issue. In the end, Coca-Cola's brand will likely overcome their handling of product tampering, but Coca-Cola saw the situation differently than their customers and suffered because they did not react swiftly to customer complaints.

There is a fine line between passion and naiveté. I know I've been in business situations where either the product division or company so believed its own story line that historically poor financial performance and business opportunities were ignored. Believing your own story line, without consideration to business reality can be a long-term unproductive way to run a business.

The old truth remains, *"It is better to cut your losses short"* than to propagate a product or service that your customers do not value. I sometimes refer to this situation, as *"The dogs are not buying the dog-food!"*

How many of us have stood in the shoes of our customers? Have we really experienced business dealings with our company and discussed issues in a brutally honest manner? Investors are quite pragmatic about where they invest their money. Customers, almost always have a choice as well. Is your company easy to do business with? Did your customers have a good *out of the box* experience with your product? In the communications industry, technology is moving so quickly and in some instances so commoditized, complexity is the name of the game and solutions are not readily apparent. Every executive in every company in the world should be required to experience his or her product or service from their customer's perspective. Only then does what you see, match your customers reality.

---

*Strong product and service feedback linkages are necessary in order to understand customers' perception of value*

---

 ### *How do we know what we do not understand?*

Many people in business are absolutely terrible at listening and understanding their customers. The Information Age is all about time, speed and productivity. The Information Age bombards us with too much information and there is too little time to digest what it means. How can a business possibly know what customers want if it does not take the time to understand customer needs? What need is your product or service fulfilling? Try asking that question every time you sit through a product review session and enjoy the hemming and hawing!

Electronic commerce is a key issue facing most businesses today. Jack Welch of General Electric sees e-commerce changing everything. In a *Fortune Magazine* interview he said, *"It will change relationships with employees. You will have to lead with ideas, not by controlling information. It will change relationships with customers. Customers will see everything. It will change relationships with suppliers. Suppliers will supply GE on the Internet or they won't do business with GE."*

Global competitors, who get it right, accurately understand their customer needs. Truly great product or service companies embed *customer understanding* in their culture because they know it is the key to long-term business success. So how do they do it? What is the magic formula for understanding?

It is really quite simple:

1) Take the time to be an active listener in everything you do.
2) Make the time to ask good questions that enables understanding.
3) Be relentless in the pursuit of bridging the perception-reality gap.

---

*A **World's Best Value**™ company takes time to listen, understand and relentlessly bridge the perception-reality gap*

---

## World's Best Value™

 *Valuing cultural differences*

I've been conducting business in the global marketplace for nearly 20 years and I am often asked what are the keys to success?  Do you need to speak multiple languages?  Does it help to study international business in business school?  What is the key to success?

In my experience, the key differentiator for success and failure is to be a *good listener*!  Ask questions.  Be open to your own shortcomings and cultural insensitivity. Peter Senge says, *"To be a real learner is to be ignorant and incompetent.  Not many top executives are up for that."*  In the end, global commerce is about people doing business with people.  I find it stimulating to be around people who have had different life and business experiences than I have.  You realize that all humanity has the same basic needs, drivers and motivations.  It is human nature!

I continue to be amazed at how culturally insensitive most of us are with people of different nationalities.  I was watching a documentary on British Broadcasting Corporation ("BBC") in the United Kingdom, about the Asian culture in Britain.  The BBC was being rather self-inspecting about its own reporting and growing tolerance of the Indian national population that began to immigrate to the U.K. in the 1970s.  Similarly, a self-inspection by many people in the United States would show cultural insensitivity to Asian, Latin American and African American cultures.  Cultural diversity is everywhere.

In a global economy, especially during the Information Age,

cultural diversity should be valued, not opposed. Worldwide talent pools exist in the far corners of the globe and global corporations are seeking diversity. A cornerstone of AT&T's culture is *synergy*.

AT&T's global alliance with BT is based on synergy to provide advanced communications services to multinational customers around the world. Nortel is communicating its view of synergy in *"How the world shares ideas"* media campaign. *Synergy is a powerful energy force that builds on differences.*

We have all heard the phrase *"one plus one equals three."* Synergy creates more than the sum of its parts. The same is true for cultural differences! It is a powerful concept to be valued.

---

*A **World's Best Value**™ company understands*
*cultural differences are a powerful force that create*
*synergy and benefits customers*

---

# *World's Best Value*™ **Plan**
## Perception is Reality?

Objective: Create a communications environment that manages perceptions.

Priorities:

1) Value perception as a factor for market messaging.

2) Develop an integrated communications plan.

3) Assess product and service messaging for acceptance.

4) Listen to customer's perceptions and respond.

5) Understand customer requirements before responding.

6) Relentlessly bridge the perception-reality gap.

7) Value cultural differences.

8) Find communications synergy based on differences.

9) Value global diversity and translate to customer benefits.

10) Measure perceptions and improve messaging.

# Chapter 7

## TQM is a Tool — That's All!

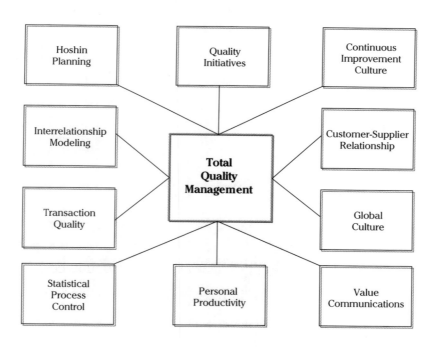

### TQM is a Tool — That's All!

 *Hoshin planning in a competitive world*

The Total Quality Management (TQM) movement began with Dr. Edward Deming after World War II in Japan. In the 1960s, *"Made in Japan,"* meant *cheap.* Today it means *quality.* Philip Crosby and others have made a good living building on the TQM model and hundreds of books have been written on the subject during the past 20 years. There is so much to learn. What is really important?

For my money, *Hoshin Planning* is an important planning concept that is an extremely useful tool that aligns resources with corporate strategy and business direction. It is an easy-to-use planning resource that is powerful in it's application. Hoshin planning, starts simply with an objective set out by the head of an organization — typically the chief executive officer followed by the 10 most important actions to take in support of an objective. The power in the tool is its ease of implementation and value derived from the interaction that determines the top 10 important actions in support of any objective. I have used this tool with companies such as Westell, NEC, BT, AT&T, Nortel and Fujitsu and it works. The power is in its simplicity.

For example, let's imagine a group of executives for a basketball franchise are brainstorming the most important things required to be a world-champion. They would, no doubt, come up with 50 or 60 ideas the executives believed important to create a world-championship team. In the end, a world-class franchise boils down to talent, teamwork, general management, coaching, revenue stream, commitment and ultimately winning. This would apply to any business division, corporation, government or educational institution that has goals for product and service success. A Hoshin-plan in a world-class business can be thought of as a *World's Best Value*<sup>TM</sup> plan. The *World's Best Value*<sup>TM</sup> planning summary for our hypothetical basketball franchise might look like this:

*World's Best Value*<sup>TM</sup> Basketball Franchise
*World's Best Value*<sup>TM</sup> Plan

Objective: To be a world-class organization that wins championship titles and continuously produces championship quality teams.

1) Create ownership structure for long term value.

2) Focus on organizational development.

3) Hire world-class coaching staff.

4) Create a business plan that sustains investments in talent.

5) Develop a fan-friendly culture that sustains revenue growth.

6) Build a world-class scouting organization.

7) Draft quality, high-character players and develop to potential.

8) Supplement draft with prudent use of free-agency.

9) Create a media-friendly environment for fair reporting.

10) Create a world-class concession and licensing structure.

104

## TQM is a Tool — That's All!

My final thoughts on **World's Best Value™** planning is to *USE IT, USE IT AGAIN, and USE IT EVEN MORE.* Misalignment of resources is the hallmark of mismanaged and misled companies. This powerful tool can be used at all levels and functions in a business. All of the work that goes under the top 10 items can be measured to ensure compliance with the overall objective. And, oh by the way, forget the documentation of all of the underlying processes unless it is absolutely necessary. There are no rewards for the documentation, only the results that help meet objectives!

---

*World-class companies use **World's Best Value™** planning as a powerful tool to help align resources with corporate objectives*

---

 *Quality means different things*

The problem with quality is that it typically means different things to different people. Many corporations have a heterogeneous work force that has more or less exposure to quality in their careers. For many companies, the goal of quality messaging is to expose employees to consistent reinforcing messages around quality concepts in order to effect behavioral change. Communications about quality needs to be simple.

At Ford, *Quality is Job 1*! For General Electric and Sony it is the pursuit of *zero defects*! At Motorola, you may have heard quality referred to as six-sigma or the five nines (99.999%). In many other companies it is a focus on *HIGH QUALITY*; high quality cloth-

105

ing, high quality food, high quality people. It seems to me, that consumers should be wary when a company speaks of quality as anything other than a given. Does high quality mean something different than low quality? or just plain quality?

Quality means different things to different people, wherever they may be in the world. Countries with a relatively thin manufacturing or software development base would likely not have the in-country experience to consistently produce quality from a global perspective.

I like to think of quality in terms of *best global practice*. Like everything in business, quality needs to be kept in perspective in order to have meaning. Best global practice means that processes or outcomes being measured, are relative to what is best compared to other businesses and the industry. Comparisons and learning gained by cross-industry reference, brings out the very best in our understanding of quality.

---

*Best global practices and quality initiatives*
*must be constantly communicated with employees*
*in order to create sustained customer value*

---

 **Continuous improvement means just that**

An important principle that supports total quality management is the notion of *continuous improvement*. The relentless pursuit of being better, every minute of every day is a powerful principle. It means that over time, through continuous improvement, quality predictably gets better. Think about getting better every day. General Electric, under the direction of their eclectic chairman, Jack Welch, is today going through such a transformation. GE's goals are lofty, firmly rooted in the principle of continuous improvement. If we could just apply the fundamentals of sports such as American football, to business, we would stand an improved chance at getting better every day. Football success is greatly influenced by the use of videotapes, analysis, game planning and the practice of continuous improvement.

What are the business implications of a culture that analyzes strengths and weaknesses every day? Businesses can focus on financial results and overlook opportunities for operations improvement.

I recently had a discussion with a business colleague about the importance of consensus gathering for top executives, and how that process enables more timely and cost effective business decisions. My feedback was meant to be constructive about the merits of his proposal.

His initial response to my feedback was to focus on the merits of his thinking and convincing me of his recommendation, without responding to my suggestion about consensus. I was hoping that my constructive feedback would stimulate his thinking about how to seek a better process and secure a supported decision.

Unfortunately, either because of his unwillingness to consider a different viewpoint, or my lack of clarity in communicating the need for continuous improvement, we did not have a meeting of the minds. Fortunately my colleague is very open to learning and this was an opportunity for both of us to focus on continuous improvement and move on from there. The need for continuous improvement is everywhere!

---

*Continuous improvement is a powerful principle widely adopted by organizations that want to be the best*

---

 ### The power of interrelationship modeling

*World's Best Value*™ companies are able to put tactical business activities in *context* of corporate strategy. Every person in every company on the face of the planet can apply this notion of *context*, to every decision.

For instance, a decision to open a new financial services office in the Tokyo, Japan requires context. A simple interrelationship model that looks at the key factors related to the decision is a useful learning and communications tool. The interrelationship model for establishing an office in the United Kingdom includes the relationship between (1) competitive environment (2) customer demographics (3) communications environment (4) product portfolio (5) financial projections (6) tax structure implications (7) labor availability (8) expatriate policy (9) public transport and (10) cash considerations.

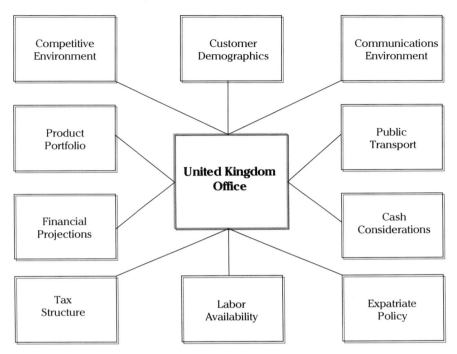

A decision such as opening a new office in the United Kingdom can be considered with a better understanding of dependencies. In effect it becomes a *mental model* that is easily understood and communicated with a wide range of constituents who have different interests. *The Mind Map* by *Tony Buzan* and *The Fifth Discipline* are good sources for better understanding relationship modeling.

The interrelationship model is a tool that enables a *shared vision* that is crucial in business decision-making. I was recently in the corporate headquarters of a Fortune 500 communications company where their shared vision was captured in a colorful series of interrelationship models. The model visually depicted key understandings about customers, competition, business values, products and partners. It was POWERFUL! Visual modeling is not an exception, as companies such as AT&T, Motorola, IBM, NEC and many others use this communications tool as part of their total quality management thinking and implementation. Businesses need to understand people are also *visual learners*. *World's Best Value™* companies that have operations in geographically diverse locations, use visual communications to transcend language, culture and written communications.

---

*Interrelationship modeling is a common quality tool used by companies that recognize the value of visual learning and understanding*

---

###  *Statistical process control is essential*

Statistical Process Control ("SPC") is an essential quality tool for manufacturing environments. One of the best books written about SPC is *Kaizen - The Key to Japan's Competitive Success* by *Masaaki Imai.* If you are not comfortable with statistics, be careful. SPC is a quantitative analysis tool that allows repetitive production activities to be quantified and expressed mathematically in order to establish a baseline for continuous improvement.

SPC can be applied to numerous areas in the business including profit planning, customer satisfaction, just in time production, systems improvement, cross-functional management, quality deployment, leadership and corporate culture commitment.

I have been part of organizations that tried to extrapolate SPC to non-manufacturing organizations with, quite frankly, mixed results. The science of SPC is not always easily or happily adopted by functions that place importance on creativity and interrupt driven business activities. Sales and marketing, for instance, do not naturally follow this science. Manufacturing and customer service do however. The key is finding the right value for it's use in your business and not force-feed a science that is misfit for use.

When determining where to implement SPC, a good rule of thumb is to look at transaction-based activities. If there is a large number of transactions involved, such as automotive assembly, durable goods manufacturing, call center transactions etc., then SPC is a candidate for use. It provides useful quantitative information and enables a transaction-based process to become a controlled process. It is important to consolidate the science of SPC to those fundamentals that are important. The key here is to develop broad usage. I think it is fair to say, not everyone involved in transaction-based activities have degrees in math or statistics.

Business areas for improvement that can benefit from *Kaizen* activities include:

- Manpower utilization
- Transaction methodology
- Time optimization
- Facilities utilization
- Manufacturing efficiency
- Materials efficiency
- Inventory management
- Production optimization

---

*A **World's Best Value**™ company implements statistical process control wherever repetitive transactions occur in business*

---

 **TQM is NOT a program!**

Total Quality Management ("TQM") is a way of doing business. Too many companies refer to TQM as a program. My experience with programs is they have a start and a finish. If TQM is a way of doing business, underpinned by **World's Best Value**™ planning, best global practices, statistical process control and interrelationship modeling, then it cannot, by definition, have a start and a finish.

**World's Best Value**™ companies each have a quality discipline and culture that transcends everything they do. Commitment for TQM begins with the shareowners, supported by the board and executive management team. If you do not see such a commitment in your company, ask why? Be part of the solution, and if all else fails, work for someone who understands the importance and value of TQM.

Individuals can often find their TQM training is a life-changing experience. Individual quality expectations outside of the business environment only increase as we learn and experience more about TQM. A word to the wise is to forewarn your friends and family. They will see a marked difference in you and your transformation into a quality thinker. Imagine how efficient the world would be if we applied TQM to our daily living.

---

*TQM is a business life-style and culture that
enables companies to develop and continuously serve
customers in a globally competitive environment*

---

 **Pick up the paper from the floor**

Speaking of implementing TQM in our daily living, I want to share a personal, but important, life-style change that occurred to me over 10 years ago. As I was experiencing quality as a science, for the first time, I became so enamored with its business and life usage that I started to notice changes in my daily living. My expectation of retail and service establishments became different. It was no longer acceptable for me as a consumer to accept anything other than a quality product that met product specifications and my own expectations. I am sure for a while, I was not easy to deal with, other than the fact I became consistent in my expectations of *fair value* for money.

113

A fundamental of TQM is the *customer-supplier* relationship. Simply, we can think of every transaction in terms of a customer-supplier relationship. We have all been exposed to such sayings as *"garbage in-garbage out"* in the computer business or *"only as good as the blocking"* in competitive football. The message is that every transaction or process has a supplier and a customer.

If we extend the customer-supplier principle to human relationships or mankind's relationship with the environment, it can cause a fundamental shift in our thinking. If we are grumpy to our family, why should we expect our family to be happy? If we litter the environment, why should we expect anything other than pollution? If a lineman in football misses a blocking assignment, why would we expect a play to be successful or efficient team play?

So the next time you are walking in your home, business or community, and you see a piece of paper littered on the floor; pick it up! When you do, you will know that TQM is taking root and applied to your everyday living.

---

*TQM can have a fundamental impact in*
*our business and personal lives*

---

 **Your customers want value, save the statistics**

In summary, customers of **World's Best Value**™ companies are looking for one thing — value! Ultimately, customers expect products that work at a price consistent with value provided. As companies begin their never-ending TQM journey, there is a natural inclination to measure progress, which is of course a fundamental premise of TQM. Unfortunately, what happens in the measurement process is to focus on process, as opposed to the end result. Companies view success or failure based on statistical progress, not necessarily customer satisfaction.

GTE, Bell Atlantic, AT&T and others look at quality measurements from their suppliers as criteria for vendor selection. This kind of business behavior reinforces statistical measurements, which may or may not yield expected product value. It is a very good place to start, but many companies look at *blending* statistics in order to come up with a customer satisfaction composite that de-emphasizes statistical analysis in any one area.

*World's Best Value™* companies understand TQM is a *tool* and statistics are a *barometer* that measures progress. Statistics are important but they are not the end result. *World's Best Value™* companies find a way to put statistics in context and encourage their employees to use statistics as a vehicle to communicate hopefully, progress. Cisco, Motorola, Lucent and Nortel do a particularly good job in this area. These companies and other market leaders committed to quality, are able to translate statistics to meaningful customer value.

*World's Best Value™* companies have a sixth sense of putting business perspectives around statistical analysis. In the end, companies are measured on profitability, the ultimate statistic!

---

*A **World's Best Value™** company uses statistics
to communicate value for their customers*

---

# *World's Best Value™* Plan
## Total Quality Management is a Tool – That's All!

Objective: Utilize total quality management tools that add value to the business.

Priorities:

1) Use *World's Best Value™* planning to align resources.

2) Constantly communicate quality initiatives.

3) Implement a continuous improvement culture.

4) Use interrelationship modeling for learning.

5) Implement statistical process control.

6) Use statistical process control for planning activities.

7) Use TQM as a tool to improve personal productivity.

8) Use TQM statistics to communicate value to customers.

9) Use TQM to improve customer-supplier relationships.

10) Make TQM a culture that serves global customers.

# Chapter 8

# Products and Services are Only the Beginning

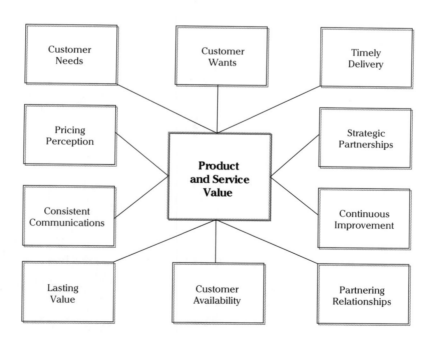

### Products and Services are Only the Beginning

 ***Customers want what THEY want***

I continue to be surprised that too many companies sell products and services that do not meet customer needs. All too often, this situation is the result of legacy products that do not evolve to meet customer requirements. How does this happen?

Products that do not meet customer requirements are usually the result of inefficient product definition, development and cycle-time processes that cause problems for new product and service introduction. What are the implications of these issues? If companies are unable to rectify their inefficiencies, then competitive products, services and new companies will fill the void and serve customer needs.

We do not live in an ideal world where new products and services appear easily or always on time. However, ***World's Best Value™*** companies predictably and consistently get it right. They have sustaining power. General Electric, Sony and Philips know how to create and deliver products and services that customers want. They build products that are based on their technological know-how and their capabilities. They uniquely anticipate customer needs. In the mid-1980s the world was operating largely on mainframe and mini computers. Individual workers had distributed terminals that shared CPU time on the computer. None of the information was shared and applications were limited. Apple, Microsoft, Intel and IBM have led a revolution to individual computing and expanded applications development. These companies took advantage of technology shifts and anticipated customers' needs.

---

*Customers expect a **World's Best Value™** company*
*to anticipate their needs and provide*
*products and services that they want*

---

 ### When THEY want it

In the Internet economy there is something known as *Internet time*. Internet time is fast — at the speed of communications. The Internet is changing everything. Businesses win or lose based on how fast they move to address changing market conditions. In the communications industry, I refer to it as a 10:1 experience. For every one year of experience, it feels like 10. That is good and bad. The good part is the learning, growth and development opportunities. The bad part is those who do not move fast enough often lose.

Customers want what they want — when they want it. The customer's world is changing. The competitive environment is complex and threatens the very existence of business. For the foreseeable future, industries will be at a crossroads as the world shifts from the industrial and computer age to the Information Age. Companies we know today may or may not be in existence tomorrow. So speed is essential.

Think about consumers and their involvement with the Internet. They want access to be streamlined and consumer friendly. They want to see content in a way they can understand with minimum interaction time. AOL, Yahoo, Excite and others are making it easier and faster for consumers and businesses to interact

120

with the Internet and each other. These companies have anticipated customers needs and are providing them what they want,
WHEN they want it.

---

*A **World's Best Value**™ company provides products
and services to customers on a timely basis*

---

 *At a good price*

I remember a time when high value meant high price. An
interesting phenomenon happened in the 1990s. The quality of
goods and services improved significantly in almost every industry in the world. Sony used to be able to get a price premium for
consumer electronic products. Lexus used to be able to charge
a price premium on its luxury sedans. Branding, for example,
does help promote higher pricing but the reality in the Information Age is that quality is expected and customers want products
and services at a good price.

The impact of this can be significant for businesses and
their corporate strategy. It can cause niche-market competitors
to seek mass-market opportunities and vice versa. The *value-
price gap* is narrowing and customers expect value pricing. Frac-
tions of any currency can make a big difference in mass market
pricing.

Lexus competitors have improved their quality and the perceived quality difference between a Lexus and Cadillac, for example, has decreased. Consumers are not always as willing to

pay the price differential. My own experience with Lexus is they are now more willing to negotiate price to get the deal done. Consumers ultimately benefit when competition drives up value and lowers prices.

Electronic commerce is redefining price competitiveness. Sears has been steadily loosing market share to competitors like Home Depot, Lowe's, Circuit City, Target and Wal-Mart. Sears is finally stepping up to its market share erosion. Sears boldly predicts it will become the definitive on-line source for the home. Sears plans to start selling appliances, parts and tools on its web site, followed by other lines of business. The on-line marketing budget at Sears in 1999 was estimated at $100 million.

At the other end of the value-spectrum, Christie's, the international auction house, is launching a redesign of its Internet strategy that will eventually create an online bidding venue for every one of the company's auctions. Value is everywhere!

---

*Products and services must be available at a good price as perceived by the customer*

---

 **Best value**

*Best Value* is a choice of words that I find exciting and at times frustrating. There is nothing in business more emotional or anecdotal. I remember making a presentation at an industry conference in London on the topic of *Broadband Access Technologies and our Digital Future*. At the end of my presentation, during the discussion and question phase, an industry analyst asked me

## *Products and Services are Only the Beginning*

for my future projection of equipment pricing for a broadband access technology called digital subscriber line. I smiled and asked him what he would want the price to be. The individual, who has since become a very good friend and respected colleague, answered, *"I don't know what the price is, but it has to be lower than whatever you are projecting!"* Such is life in the communications industry. It is a challenge to create and sell value.

On a related front, *price wars* for food products are beginning to show up in European countries. These price wars provide a useful model for understanding value. Wal-Mart has acquired ASDA in the United Kingdom. As a result, Tesco, Sainsbury's and Waitrose are scrambling to be competitive. Using Eurodollars as the base currency, let's do an analysis of price for a pound of ham and determine which one is the *best value*. To be completely accurate, we need to also understand the percentage of water added to the meat product to determine the best price for a pound of ham:

|  | Store A | Store B | Store C |
|---|---|---|---|
| Price for lb. of ham | 4.00 | 4.10 | 4.25 |
| Percentage of water added | 10% | 5% | 2% |
| Price of diluted ham | 4.44 | 4.32 | 4.34 |
| **Best Value** | **3rd** | **1st** | **2nd** |

## World's Best Value™

Best price does not necessarily mean best value. It is a challenge for companies to clearly communicate and set expectations with respect to pricing. Companies need to meet their customer requirements for the product or service they want, when they want it, at the best price.

---

*A **World's Best Value™** company knows how to consistently create and communicate value for customers*

---

 ### And they want it to last

In the 1970s consumers were used to products that did not last. Quality was not an expectation in many industries. Many products, such as automobiles were purchased with *planned obsolescence* in mind. There was a very large gap between high quality and low quality products and services. At that time, global competition was, in many respects, at its infancy. Customers had little choice but to accept what was available.

The worldwide quality revolution began in the 1980s. In the communications industry, for example, customers began to have choices as regulators introduced legislation to encourage competition. The break-up of AT&T's long distance and local access business started a tidal wave of similar regulatory actions around the world, resulting in more choice for better quality products and services at a reduced price. As mentioned, quality was taking root in the 1980s and consumers began to expect durable goods and services to last.

### Products and Services are Only the Beginning

The 1990s marked a transition from companies being multinational to being more global in their thinking and actions. Leading global companies such as Ford, British Airways, IBM and General Electric became very attuned to customer needs on a country-by-country basis. They learned that customers want the products that they want, when they want it at a good price. Customers expect long-lasting value in the products and services. The bar keeps getting higher in a globally competitive marketplace.

---

*Customers expect products and services to have lasting value*

 ### Where were you when I needed you?

We have established that quality products and services are only the beginning. Customers want what they want, when they want it, at a good price and to have lasting value. But what happens when something goes wrong? How do *World's Best Value™* companies respond to issues that occur in the product supply chain or when the value of the product or service is in question?

It is not uncommon in the communications industry to have service issues that included network, transmission (wireless, wire line, fiber, satellite) and customer premise devices (router, modem, computers). Customers expect the service provider to take ownership for problems when they occur. For example, high-speed digital service customers are demanding service up time commitments in the range of 99 percent or higher!

Internet communications has eliminated most of the customer service excuses that suppliers use when customers ask for help. Diagnostic tools are plentiful. Problem identification is more timely and cost effective.

Customer service can be extremely responsive in an Internet-based environment. If a customer has to ask, *"Where were you when I needed you?"* your company may not have to worry about that customer again. The customer will look for a new supplier if you are not there in good and difficult times.

---

*Customers expect suppliers to be there when
they need them in good and difficult times*

---

 ***Partnership or supplier***

I would like to share some insights about the kind of relationship your company has with your key customer(s). Michael Macoby of Macoby Associates, a highly respected consultant to the information technology industry, hosted a conference on the topic of partnering in the mid-1990s in Washington D.C. I had the opportunity to participate in the conference along with several business associates and executives from the banking, mining, chemical and communications industries.

I had a chance to lead a group through an exercise that has since become a time-proven model for thinking about customer relationships and articulating the kind of behavior and characteristics present at each level in the *partnering model.*

126

### *Products and Services are Only the Beginning*

The model looks at a continuum of business relationships including:

**Partnering Model**

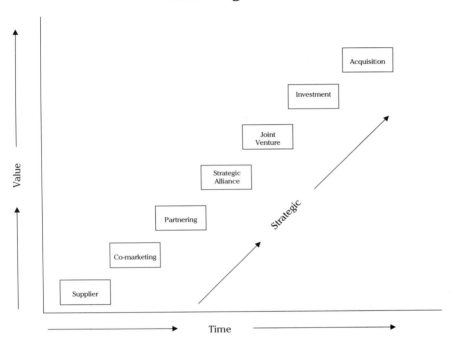

A *supplier* relationship is typically a buy-sell relationship

*Co-marketing* is when two companies reference sell each other's products or services

*Partnering* is a dependency on each other where common goals exist

*Strategic alliance* is a close alignment between two companies at a strategic level

127

*Joint venture* is an economic investment by each company in each other

*Investment* is a strategic interest resulting in typically minority equity ownership

*Acquisition* is a strategic interest resulting in full equity ownership

The key learning from this model is to understand business relationships in the continuum and deliver expectations associated with each level of partnering. This kind of thinking takes the supply of goods and services to a much different level. It becomes an excellent teaching tool to gain shared understanding and culture.

---

A ***World's Best Value*™** *company understands and derives value from partnering relationships with customers*

---

# *World's Best Value™* Plan
## Products and Services Are Only The Beginning

Objective: Enhance the product and services value provided to customers.

Priorities:

1) Anticipate customer product and service needs.

2) Provide products and services customers want.

3) Provide timely delivery of products and services.

4) Provide good pricing as perceived by customers.

5) Consistently communicate value to customers.

6) Produce products and services with lasting value.

7) Be available for customers in difficult times.

8) Develop partnering relationships that add value.

9) Extend supplier relationships to partnering if strategic.

10) Continuously improve product and service value.

# Chapter 9

## Lead, Follow or Fail

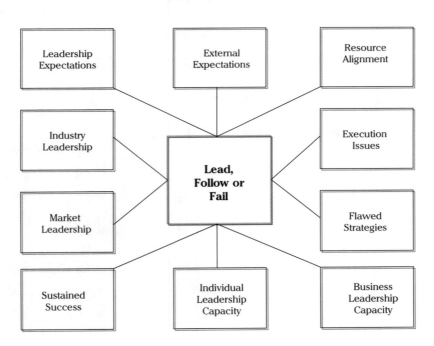

## Lead, Follow or Fail

 ### *What kind of company are you?*

There are several hundred thousand people employed at Lucent Technologies, the largest communications equipment supplier in the world. It would be an interesting exercise to interview each employee separately and ask the question, *"What kind of company is Lucent Technologies?"*

Responses would likely range from the company mission statement to *"I'm not really sure"*. Or perhaps it would be the company advertising, *"We make things that make communications work"*. The same example could be true for other large companies, start-ups and medium size businesses. One of the greatest leadership challenges facing companies is to align people and organizations.

General Electric has made it known to its leadership team, shareowners and customers, it intends to be a leader in it's chosen market segments. Cisco Systems, Motorola and other best in class companies have similar mandates. Cisco, for example, focuses heavily on mergers and acquisitions to respond to rapidly changing customer expectations. John Chambers says companies that emerge as industry leaders, will be those who understand how to partner and acquire.

Years ago, a former business associate of mine who had previously worked at Bell Laboratories and 3Com, shared his view on microelectronics technology, called the *Law of Absorption*. The law of absorption principle has to do with increased processing and transmission software functionality being absorbed into multipurpose digital signal processors. The principle is an

131

important one for companies that design application specific software not embedded in digital signal processors. It basically means that the value of communications and processing software must increase in value or be absorbed by other processing technologies. The same analogy holds true for businesses.

The reason that **World's Best Value**™ companies choose a path of leadership is they know they must either grow, be absorbed (acquisition), or go out of business. **World's Best Value**™ companies must either be a market leader, develop a niche market and dominate that segment, or if unable to secure a leadership position, ultimately withdraw from the market or fail as a business.

---

A **World's Best Value**™ company widely
communicates leadership expectations

---

 ### *To be a market leader*

At the root of every strategic planning session should be the question, *"What kind of business do you want to be?"* It is a simple question to ask, and very difficult to answer. Many companies find it difficult to make the necessary commitment of resources in order to align implementation with vision. Misalignment is probably the single greatest issue that faces leadership teams in both public and privately held companies.

For those companies that answer, *"We want to be a market leader"*, the challenges remain ahead. To be a market leader requires alignment between the board, leadership team, all employees and shareowners. It requires alignment with strategic planning, operations planning, tactical execution and results. Market leadership takes cash for investments. Market leadership takes a commitment to deal with a business environment inside and outside companies' control. Market leadership takes personal leadership at all levels within a company.

Why is it that companies and people fail to consistently take up the mantle of market leadership? Is it fear of competition? Is it fear of failure? Failed market leadership is, in my experience, a lack of complete understanding of all of the things necessary to be successful. It is often misalignment and under-commitment of resources.

---

*Market leaders make the necessary alignment and commitment of resources for business success*

---

 ### Social responsibilities of a leader

So much has been written about social responsibilities of corporations. It may not be surprising to know, that all businesses do not accept their social responsibilities. The pursuit of profitability at any cost can overshadow *"doing the right thing"* in communities where companies do business. It is a real dilemma for companies to do the right thing, because there is so much need in the local communities. People tend to think that *big corporations* make big money and should give it away. The reality is that corporations, especially publicly traded corporations, have a complex set of responsibilities and are driven by a need to increase shareowner value.

My own experience in this area is to think of social responsibilities much like we think about *Maslow's hierarchy of needs*. It is, for most people, difficult to reach out beyond their own needs until they have food, shelter, clothing and security. The same is true for corporations that find it difficult to give back to the community until profitability, growth and return on investments are consistently achieved. There are exceptions, of course. AT&T, Ford, DuPont, General Motors, Microsoft and others generously give, and in many instances are setting up a legacy for giving. The $17 billion Gates Foundation is a good example.

The richest man in the world, Bill Gates, has set up the largest gift giving foundation in the world. His passion is putting the power of computing and access to the Internet in the hands of as many people as possible with particular focus on education. Notwithstanding the ideals of a better world, if more people have access to computers and technology, it benefits companies like Microsoft. It is a win-win business proposition.

A friend and colleague of mine, David Sibbald, influenced my life several years ago. David is Chairman and CEO of Atlantech Technologies, a communications software company located in Glasgow, Scotland. We were at church together one beautiful summer morning reflecting on a number of worldly issues after the service. I asked my colleague what he wanted to do with the wealth he would create when he either took his company public or sold it?  He comfortably responded, *"I want to make a lot of money and give it all away!"*  Mind you, at the time my friend was all of 35 years old and was already thinking about what he wanted to do with his anticipated good fortune.  His vision of the social responsibilities of business and market leaders inspired me to set up a charitable-giving company, Investech Foundation.  I have been fortunate to fund the foundation directly and through the generosity of friends and business colleagues around the world.  My foundation focuses on education, athletic and community development gift giving.

Social responsibilities exist at the individual level.  It happens in small and large companies.  It happens in every corner of the world.  ***World's Best Value™*** companies willingly accept their social responsibilities as leaders and set examples for their industries and communities.

---

*Market leaders willingly accept their social responsibilities and lead their industry and communities by example*

---

 ### Being second can be first

Is it necessary for companies to be first in their market segment or industry?  The pursuit of being number one is deeply entrenched in capitalistic cultures and western society.   In the United States we see that kind of attitude in educational and athletic pursuits, sometimes to the point of being unhealthy.  Corporate recruiters for college graduates often place a high priority on being first in class, overlooking the well-rounded students who find ways to balance education with social and athletic endeavors. Can anyone remember who came second in the last Olympic 100m race? How about who came second in batting average in the American League of Major League Baseball? Who placed second in the 1998 World Cup?

The psychology of being second is really one that says you have lost. My experience says this attitude is not based on full understanding of the power and value of being second. Let me illustrate. Is it better or different to be a *runner-up* than *second place*? How about *finalist* as opposed to second place? For me, runner-up and finalist are more positive and self-effacing than second place. It means that you have gotten to the finals. It means that you were in a position to be the best.

I am not advocating that anyone be other than the best they can be as an individual or a company. The facts are that countless successful companies who are not first in their market segments yet still provide **World's Best Value**™ products and services. Avis has created a brand for being second in their industry; "*We Try Harder*".

Rolls Royce is doing quite well in a jet-engine market dominated by General Electric. Panasonic is not the largest consumer electronics company in the world, but it is a household name and competes effectively against Philips and Sony. Being second, in many instances, can be a competitive advantage that helps create differentiation and enables long-term business success.

*Countless companies are first to create sustained business success by being second in their chosen market segments*

###  Do something — or be left behind

A fundamental principle of **World's Best Value™** companies is a recognition that existing and emerging competitors around the world are scheming every day to win market share. John Chambers, Chief Executive Officer of Cisco Systems has been very public about Cisco's *virtual closing* of the financial and management accounts on any given business day during the month, quarter, or year. What is the impact of a virtual closing? It is a powerful advantage for Cisco. The worldwide leader in data networking is doing something about maintaining its competitive advantage. In this example, Cisco will be able to provide its management teams around the world with virtually real time information to help them run their business and compete.

Let's stay with the Cisco example. How does Cisco plan to maintain its market leadership position in nearly every aspect of data networking? Cisco is going to continue to invest in core technologies and acquire new companies, technologies and people to fuel future growth. In the last half of the 1990s, Cisco invested more than $19 billion in nearly 50 networking and software companies. It is a winning model. Investors love Cisco, and if imitation is the greatest form of flattery, watch how Lucent Technologies, Nortel, Alcatel and others choose to grow and develop their businesses over time. Where appropriate, they are following the Cisco model.

Success does not just happen. Leadership requires growth and development each and every day. Professional sports are a great teaching tool for business. How has Manchester United built arguably the finest club soccer team in the world? Why did the Boston Celtics dominate professional basketball in the 1950s and 1960s? What is Tiger Woods doing to maintain his growing dominance in world golf? Why has Pete Sampras consistently been the best player in men's tennis during the past decade? The consistent theme for all of these winning people and teams is that they do something to improve themselves every day. They embody continuous improvement. *Challenges and setbacks are embraced as opportunities for learning and improvement.* High-performance people and companies know if they do not do something to improve, they will be left behind and being left behind is unacceptable.

---

*Market leaders and winning people continuously improve themselves each day for fear of being left behind*

---

 *Nobody likes a loser*

Let's define losing in a different context. Losing *is failure to be successful in your chosen field of endeavor.* So many times, failure is a function of never acknowledging or understanding the requirements for success. Sometimes people and companies compete because they have always done so, but failed to recognize the requirements for success.

### *Lead, Follow or Fail*

Strategy is about making choices.  Strategy is choosing what to do and not to do.  It is about companies saying no to activities that are inconsistent with a chosen strategy.  This is important because it provides context for decisions that lead to winning and losing.  It is better to not compete at all, than to compete and lose without a commitment to win.  Losing is a waste of precious human and capital resources.   Is it losing when a business strategy dictates withdraw from competition?  I would argue no, it is a statement of choice regarding allocation of resources.

For example, NEC, Japan's largest personal computer manufacturer has dramatically scaled back its personal computer operations in the light of significant competition from Dell, Compaq, Toshiba and Gateway.  NEC, has chosen to specialize in the PC market and has formed an Internet services alliance with Oracle, Hewlett Packard and others to develop its Internet business.  The companies will combine their software technologies and services capabilities to provide customers with e-commerce business solutions.

Why do people and companies loose in the battle of competition?  The answer is often misallocation of human and capital resources.  Losing is an opportunity for learning.  It is an opportunity to critically assess what it takes to be successful.  All too often losing and the resulting blame placed on people, is only part of the problem.  Losing is really a leadership problem that starts at the top of every company and includes each person individually and collectively as a team.

## World's Best Value™

There are countless examples of business-turnarounds as a result of addressing business system problems, Apple Computer being a recent good example. The important thing to learn is that *losing is a systems problem*. Understanding the system problem is the first step toward building a winning system and success.

---

*Losing is a system problem beginning with an incomplete strategy followed by flawed execution*

---

# *World's Best Value*™ Plan
## Lead, Follow or Fail

Objective:  Establish a market leadership strategy.

Priorities:

1) Communicate leadership expectations internally.

2) Communicate leadership expectations externally.

3) Commit and align resources for business success.

4) Accept social responsibilities of industry leadership.

5) Extend market leadership to communities.

6) Create sustained success being second.

7) Improve individual capacity for leadership.

8) Improve business capacity for leadership.

9) Acknowledge losing is a result of flawed strategy.

10) Learn that losing is a result of poor execution.

# Chapter 10

## Believe with a Passion

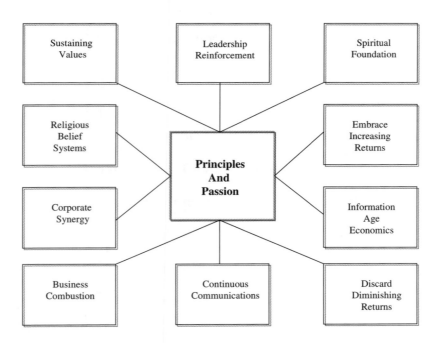

## Believe with a Passion

 ### Corporate culture is critical

When creating or leading a company that provides **World's Best Value**™ products and services, it is crucial to get the company culture right. Developing any business means bringing diverse people, cultures and resources together. This is either a huge opportunity to create shared culture or a potential for disaster. Every business has a culture. Culture usually starts with the personality of the leader and the company develops that culture over time. It has taken Jack Welch of General Electric more than 10 years to get a set of values that everyone can buy into.

So how do businesses create or modify a corporate culture? What are the things that are important to the business now and in the future? Where should a business begin? The best place to start is with a clean sheet of paper and use the **World's Best Value**™ planning tool. Remember that establishing or changing the company culture is one of the most important things that a company does. **World's Best Value**™ companies consistently and effectively change their corporate culture, when required.

Corporate cultures must be grounded in sustainable values. Successful corporate cultures must be based on principles that stand the test of time. Leaders who fashion their corporate culture must be prepared to apply the necessary focus and resources. Corporate cultures require strong belief systems. Companies must have a passion for culture creation and implementation. If you believe that there is a linkage between sustained business success and corporate culture, there is very little choice but to execute with passion.

Creating and modifying corporate cultures is an enormous change process. Enduring the change process will take the strength and conviction of the top leadership team supported by middle management and shared with all employees. It will take an unbelievable amount of communications. I spoke with a human resource executive at a Fortune 500 company recently. She told me that her company reinforces corporate culture messages no less than six times over a period of six to twelve months in order to establish understanding and a root system that takes hold and blossoms.

---

*Successful companies passionately believe in the importance of corporate culture for sustained business success*

---

###  How spiritually grounded is your company?

Have you ever noticed that companies almost always frown upon the open discussion and practice of religion in the workplace? I have often wondered why companies do not take the opposite position and encourage the pursuit of religious belief systems or spirituality, because of the profound positive impact it can have for successful companies. I have had an opportunity to build and develop successful businesses based on underlying spiritual values and principles based on service. My extensive worldwide travels during the past 10 years tell me that consistently successful companies almost *always* have strong spiritual belief systems or service principles at their core.

144

### *Believe with a Passion*

A strong spiritual belief system is not necessarily about being Muslim, Protestant, Jewish, Catholic, Hindu or other specific religious faiths. It is rather a strong underlying belief system in something greater than earthly pursuits. It is a passion for serving that comes from belief in a higher being. It is a passion for helping that often, but not always, comes from a religious belief system. I have wondered if companies without a strong belief in a higher being can command the kind of leadership required to lead businesses, markets and create value. The answer is absolutely yes; as long as that person or company's culture is strongly rooted in serving and helping customers be successful.

Spiritual foundation is a terrific place to start to build and develop a business with passion. Passion should be nurtured and reinforced constantly. So much the better if the spiritual foundation has religious ramifications. The diversity of religious beliefs with a common thread of spirituality can be powerful. It can be synergistic and create high levels of energy. It can sustain people and businesses in good and difficult times. It can be a common thread that ties together the leading people and businesses that provide *World's Best Value™* products and services.

---

*Businesses built on spiritual foundations can*
*have sustaining value*

---

145

### *One plus one equals three*

I love the phrase *"one plus one equals three."* It is irreverent at one level and profound at another. It solicits all kinds of positive and negative comments left unexplained. Interestingly enough, the phrase can cause a negative reaction because it can sound trite and flippant. Any time the sum of the parts is greater than the whole, you have a winner.

The phrase one plus one equals three is sometimes referred to as *synergy*. Synergy may be a bit limiting here, as I think of synergy as creating value from differences. There is power in synergy but perhaps not the same as one plus one equals three. I like to think of this phenomenon more like *business combustion*. Combustion is a powerful combination of air and fuel that creates energy, motion and power. Business combustion is a combination of people, values and processes that create energy, drive and powerful results for customers and shareowners.

Business combustion is the dream of merger-makers when companies are put together to create powerful world forces. When Citibank and Travelers Group combined in 1998 to form one of the largest financial services company in the world, the leaders of the two companies were looking for business combustion. They were looking to create drive, energy and a powerful industry force. Citigroup is only getting stronger with the hiring of former Treasury Secretary, Robert Rubin. Rubin became a director, chairman of the executive committee and member of the new office of the chairman. He has a well-earned reputation as a conciliator and should provide world-class leadership.

### Believe with a Passion

Business combustion, interestingly enough, does not just happen. Businesses, like engine technology, must have the right environment for combustion. Merged companies sometimes fall short because there is a disconnect between vision and implementation. How do businesses enable human potential to blossom? How do they get the most out of the combination of people, processes and performance? It takes planning, implementation and communication.

---

*Companies that create an environment for "business combustion" reap the rewards of sustained business success*

---

 ### The law of increasing returns

One of the most powerful learning's about the Information Age is that it has turned traditional economic theory upside down. Many of today's business leaders have grown up in an educational environment that preached the principles of *law of diminishing returns*. Simply said, diminishing returns mathematically show the interrelationship between uses of resources and capital. It reinforces the sum total of the parts *IS* the whole. In the Information Age, nothing could be farther from the truth!

In the Information Age, the *law of increasing returns* is changing the world. We can thank Bill Gates, Rich McGinn, Andy Grove and John Chambers for creating a business and communications environment that is changing the face of nations. Increasing returns means that when you provide a few people with

147

the right applications software, computing and communications technologies, these people can effectively compete against much bigger and stronger competitors. Increasing returns means the implementation of technology that significantly changes the human resource and process management in businesses. It means doing more with less!

The law of increasing returns has allowed companies like Microsoft, America On Line and Cisco to become leading companies in their chosen market segments within the past decade. The market capitalization of these companies exceeds the wealth of many nations. The marketplace and government institutions feel the worldwide influence from these and other leading Information Age companies. The speed of their development and business growth has been awe-inspiring. These companies and others like them that have embraced the *law of increasing returns* are providing significant value for their customers, shareowners and the world.

---

*The law of increasing returns is a powerful new*
*Information Age economics that is changing the world*

---

# *World's Best Value™* **Plan**
## Believe With a Passion

Objective:   Create a company culture based on principles and passion.

Priorities:

1) Establish a culture based on sustaining values.

2) Top leadership team must consistently reinforce culture.

3) Create a spiritual foundation for business passion.

4) Openly embrace different belief systems and religions.

5) Create corporate synergy.

6) Implement culture that creates *business combustion.*

7) Continuously plan, implement and communicate culture.

8) Discard culture that embraces *law of diminishing returns.*

9) Embrace culture that believes in *law of increasing returns.*

10) Embrace speed and economics of the Information Age.

# Chapter 11

## Strategy is No Accident

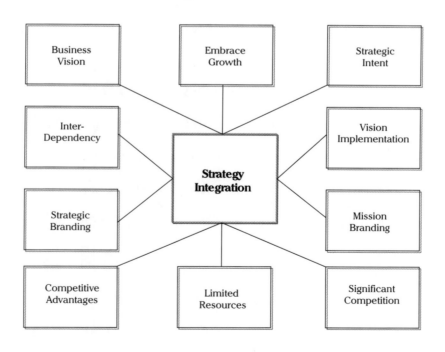

Business
Vision

Embrace
Growth

Strategic
Intent

Inter-
Dependency

Strategy
Integration

Vision
Implementation

Strategic
Branding

Mission
Branding

Competitive
Advantages

Limited
Resources

Significant
Competition

### *Strategy is No Accident*

 ### *What should we be when we grow up?*

The law of survival is either grow, be strong, or die. In human terms, think about the fact that from the day we were born, there was no guarantee we would live or be successful. Survival is a humbling reality.

In business terms, *growth is a matter of corporate survival*. Companies must grow, be absorbed (mergers) with others or die. It is the law of the corporate jungle. The history of business is such that companies with a clear vision of their future have a much greater likelihood of achieving that future. How many times have you been in corporate strategy sessions where consensus on business direction is either extremely difficult or impossible? It is not an easy process, but it is extremely important.

In our youth, it was common to dream about *"what we wanted to be when we grew up?"* For many of us, the question about our future remains unanswered, leading to a lifetime of uncertainty, confusion and disappointment. Without clear goals and objectives, our lives can become meaningless, resulting in a day-to-day survival mode. It is not a lot of fun to live this way.

Corporations uncertain about their future have the same challenges as individuals. Companies will struggle if they cannot define and communicate their future and develop a strategy to realize their business objectives. Inconsistencies show up in financial performance, human motivation, product development and customer satisfaction. Companies without a corporate strategy are ships without rudders. They are planes without a flight plan.

151

Business circumstances can most certainly cause businesses to *reinvent* themselves or significantly shift corporate strategy and direction. The Internet creates significant challenges for corporate executives and strategic planners to put their businesses in context of a rapidly changing business environment. *E-commerce* is the buzzword of most businesses trying to fend off start-ups and new business competitors who are changing the ground rules by use of Internet technology.

Beware if your company cannot describe its business in one sentence. *"We are a transportation company"*, *"We are a global consumer goods company"*, *"We want to be an Internet travel services content company"*, all are examples of well-defined outcomes of what companies want to be when they grow up. It all starts with a well-defined and understood strategy.

---

*Corporate strategy begins with a well-understood description of what kind of business it is or wants to be*

---

##  Interdependent strategic intent

Interdependency acknowledges that parts of a system are related and important to the whole. A business is a system. Strategy, planning, financing, operations, engineering, manufacturing, sales, marketing, customer service and administration are all necessary functions for a business to operate. An efficient business system is when these functions are working well together.

*Strategic intent* is a phrase used increasingly by companies around the world that want to make strategy interdependent with its business operations. In the same way that company cultures help people and businesses make good decisions, strategic intent measures business decisions against what is strategically important to a business.

We can think of strategic intent in the same way we think about motivation and human behavior. Why does a person act in a certain way? How many times have we experienced extremely motivated people only to ask ourselves why he or she is acting in a certain way? Why do professional athletes push themselves so hard in training? Why do world-class athletes choose to be the best in the world in their profession? Answers to these questions help us understand the drive, motivation, goals and objectives of people. The same understanding is relevant in business, and is especially true in world-class companies.

Strategic intent is a powerful strategy tool that helps people and businesses define priorities and make decisions on allocation of resources. For instance, if the strategic intent of NTL, the United Kingdom's largest cable operator, is to be a market leader in voice and data-communications services in Europe, then NTL will take the necessary actions to build cable and communication infrastructures in support of their strategy. In this instance, NTL's strategic intent would permeate every business transaction and the way in which it serves its customers. Strategic intent will drive NTL to be voracious in its appetite for sources of capital to acquire and grow its business. NTL's strategic intent to be a communication services market leader will be a part of every business transaction.

The real power of strategic intent is when it is present in every function of the business. The business that has interdependent strategic intent as a culture is a functional business. Absence of strategic intent is dysfunctional. *Branding* can be a lightning rod for attention to strategic intent. Branding can communicate in simple terms, company culture and corporate strategy. BASF, for instance defines its brand as, *"We make things that make other things better."* General Electric uses *"We bring good things to life."* British Airways brands itself as *"We bring the world together."* Branding can be a powerful tool for interdependent strategic intent.

---

*Strategic intent is interdependently used in **World's Best Value™** companies across all business functions*

---

 ## Competitive advantage and differentiation

Competitive advantage and differentiation is critically important to all businesses. For start-up companies, it is essential. *Michael Porter's* book, *Competitive Advantage*, is a good reference for a detailed understanding of these concepts. Competitive advantage and competitive differentiation are the cornerstones of modern strategy development in the Information Age. ***World's Best Value™*** businesses recognize its importance and as a result spend a lot of time and attention understanding their competitive environment and how to differentiate.

## Strategy is No Accident

Why is it important to differentiate? As I mentioned, Garrick Case is one of the leading public relations executives in the communications industry. He is also a daily newspaper correspondent and journalist who sees the world from that perspective. He is quite empathetic and understanding of the time constraints of writers and editors. He believes that company communications to the media should ideally be newsworthy. With so many daily press releases that cross editors' desks, those that are seen — get the ink. Garrick likes to say, *"the more black (ink) the more green (money)."*

Think about the Internet service provider industry. UUNet, AOL, Yahoo and others almost exclusively focus on two things; *content and brand development.* Internet service providers know that they have to provide *differentiated* products and services if they are going to be successful. Ease of access and excellent customer service all are important, but the key to growth for these companies is to develop their products (content) and create a unique identity that will create and retain customers. America On Line has done a good job of creating their brand, so much so that they are the largest Internet service provider in the world. America On Line customers enjoy easy communications with each other (chat lines and instant messaging) as well as ease of navigating the Internet.

One of the fastest growing segments of the communications industry is wireless communications. Ericsson, Nokia, Qualcomm and Motorola have dominant market positions. They are challenged to *differentiate* their products in a market where

155

the handset (cell phone) is often a give-away, or heavily discounted, in order to promote use on the cellular network. The network operator or service provider often underwrites the cost of the cell phones. Cell phone suppliers must differentiate by brand recognition, quality and technology. The small size of a cell phone and ease of use are important for most cell phone users. Size and features are the result of best world practices in manufacturing and process technologies as well as advances in software and silicon integration. Given that technological advances over time are generally not sustainable, differentiation depends heavily on quality. Motorola, for example, is a world leader in creating *perceived value* from its quality practices that result in quality products and services.

Competitive advantage requires analyzing the capabilities of your business relative to other businesses in the world. For General Electric, a key competitive advantage is their GE Capital financing and leasing subsidiary. General Electric sells jet aircraft engines, advanced medical diagnostic systems and large capital project management services. These products and services can cost billions of U.S. dollars, causing GE customers to seek financing packages that defer the cost of up front capital payment requirements and back end load the costs by leasing and other creative financing packages. The traditional banking and finance industry may or may not offer competitive financial packages that meet large capital financing needs. General Electric solved that problem and along the way created a financial services company that provides GE a competitive advantage in the marketplace. The

156

creation of a differentiated competitive strategy in this example was no accident.

---

*A **World's Best Value**™ company knows how to exploit competitive advantage and differentiate by branding*

---

 ### Limited resources and competition

Japan, an island country of 120 million people, is one of the most competitive nations in the world. Only 30 percent of the landmass is inhabited and it is a country of limited natural resources such as iron ore, and land for growing food. It relies heavily on importing foods, and raw materials for its manufacturing industry. So why is it that Japan has one of the leading car manufacturing and steel producing industries in the world? Why is it that Japan is generally recognized as having one of the leading consumer electronics industries in the world? Why is it that Japan has one of the leading financial services industries in the world? Remember Japan is an island nation that was politically and industrially bankrupt after World War II.

The answer is simple, Japan has had to think and act strategically. It has had to consider, as a nation, how to exploit other countries resources. It has had to focus its intellectual capital on new industries and technologies that are not natural resource dependent. Japanese companies are generally not known for their innovation, but they are amongst the best in the world at producing cost effective products and services better than most companies and able to compete on a global basis. Japanese industry has become globally competitive because the survival of their nation was a stake.

The former Chrysler Corporation, again, is a good example of creating and implementing a successful strategy based on *limited resources* and *increased competition*. In the 1980s Chrysler Corporation was on the verge of bankruptcy. Its products were known for poor quality and they had the lowest market share of their Detroit competitors, Ford and General Motors. The turnaround story at Chrysler is well documented and a lesson for Information Age companies and industries. What lesson was learned? Chrysler reinvented itself and focused on quality and new product development. Strong financial management was important but not the difference maker. Chrysler had to win back mind share and reinvented its brand as an innovative company that produced quality transportation vehicles. The crowning jewel of their turnaround was the dedication of their multi-billion dollar research and development center outside of Detroit.

A business colleague of mine, who is Chief Technology Officer of a start-up networking company, recently discussed a complex product development issue with me. He described a customer environment that demanded multiple use of transmission and protocol technologies in products that are supplied by his company. There were no less than eight different communications protocols (the things that networking devices use to communicate across networks) and three transmission technologies (the networking engine that is based on the type of network provided by the communications service provider).

### *Strategy is No Accident*

As he was considering a staffing decision, he was concerned about the time to market and resource issues associated with this dilemma. As we talked though the problem, he spoke of a breakthrough in his thinking the previous evening. It occurred to him, that *platform commonality* was the solution. His solution was to have one hardware platform with different processor technologies that handled the transmission problem and to modularize the protocol interfaces for maximum flexibility and cost optimization. The world is in fact moving at Internet speed and simple solutions are not always obvious.

This example reminds me of Ford's world car initiative (Focus). In order to be a global competitor, Ford created an optimized car *platform* that is used around the world with engine, transmission and body style differentiation based on regional market requirements.

The key is in an environment of *limited resources* and *increased competition*, Ford and the Chief Technology Officer had to think strategically. Their respective *breakthroughs* will provide significant business value for their companies and customers.

---

*A **World's Best Value**™ company embraces an environment of limited resources and increased competition to create and execute strategic intentions*

---

# World's Best Value™

 ## The vision thing

In the 1992 general election for the United States presidency, George Bush was ridiculed for his public comments on disdain for the *"vision thing."* His response, as I recall, was related to some tough questioning from reporters on economic and foreign policy strategy. His off the cuff comments provided enormous insight into either his lack of understanding of the importance of strategy, or insensitivity to his responsibilities as leader of the western world. George Bush is an honorable man and has provided invaluable service to people in the United States, but his *vision thing* comment was the beginning of the end for his re-election campaign.

While consulting with the executive management team of a European networking company, I was asked by its Chief Executive Officer about the importance of a mission statement. On the surface it was an innocent question, but behind it was clearly a level of skepticism regarding the *mission statement* thing. My guess was that he had a bad experience with mission statements and was testing my experience in this area.

My response was that mission statements could be useful communication tools for larger organizations in geographically dispersed locations. Mission statements sometimes get caught up in *words* as opposed to the *meaning or intention* behind the words. Mission statements tend to be operational intentions. What sometimes is missing from mission statements is the *strategic intention* behind the mission statement. Strategic intent creates an environment for employees to internalize strategy and execute the mission. In summary, my response is that mission statements can be useful and do have a place in the business environment. Mission statements should be concise and ideally build brand equity for a company.

A *vision tool* that I prefer is the **World's Best Value**™ planning tool described earlier in the book. **World's Best Value**™ planning puts vision front and center in order to catch the imaginations of employees. It needs to be concise and profound in its wording and intent. The power of **World's Best Value**™ planning as a vision tool is developing the set of priorities that are described as the ten most important in the business. Describing the ten priorities forces people and companies to determine what are the most important actions a business must take to support its vision. My experience has been that **World's Best Value**™ planning works extremely well with employees and is better able to translate vision, mission and implementation than other communication tools.

Ultimately most people work for companies in order to earn a living and pursue a career filled with challenge and development opportunities. The lack of a coherent vision signals that a company may not have a bright future. If a company is unable or unwilling to share its vision with its people, chances are it does not have a vision that stands inspection.

**World's Best Value**™ companies recognize people as one of their most important assets and consistently communicate vision on a regular basis to gained shared commitment. The

## World's Best Value™

Andersen Consulting Economist Intelligence Unit ran a survey that concluded 75 percent of executives worldwide rate human performance ahead of productivity and technology in strategic importance. 80 percent of those same executives said that by 2010, attracting and retaining people will be the number one force in strategy.

---

*Vision is vitally important to communicate
with employees and customers*

---

# *World's Best Value*™ Plan
## Strategy is No Accident

Objective:  Make strategy an integrated part of the business.

Priorities:

1) Create a well-understood business vision.

2) Embrace growth as a matter of business survival.

3) Create and communicate strategic intent.

4) Implement strategic intent interdependently.

5) Create and differentiate the strategic brand.

6) Exploit competitive advantages.

7) Strategize in an environment of limited resources.

8) Strategize in an environment of significant competition.

9) Openly embrace company vision.

10) Widely communicate and brand company mission.

# Chapter 12

## Create Conditions for Success

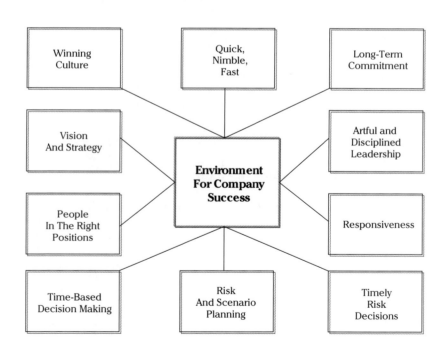

## Create Conditions for Success

 *Play to win*

Companies that provide **World's Best Value**™ products and services consistently create the right conditions for their business to be successful. An outcome from this philosophy is an expectation of *competing to win*. In the Information Age the stakes are high for businesses if they do not move fast.

In 1999, The Center for Research in Electronic Commerce at the University of Texas figured the Internet economy was valued at over $300 billion, including online sales of industrial and consumer goods and services, as well as equipment and service to support electronic commerce. Commerce on the Internet will create significant obstacles and opportunities for business. Entire industries including computing, electronics, telecommunications, financial services, retailing, energy and travel face tremendous upheaval that threatens the very existence of many companies.

In the Information Age, competition is not an intellectual pursuit, it is a matter of corporate survival. Nothing is more exciting than competition on a level playing field. The Information Age playing field is equal, primarily due to the availability of information and communication technologies. In fact, smaller companies can often have a competitive advantage. Small means quick, nimble and fast. Big usually means size, scale and stability.

**World's Best Value**™ companies know that it is not good enough just to compete. Further study of the success models at

165

## *World's Best Value™*

Wal-Mart, Southwest Airlines and Amazon.com show a corporate culture that focuses on success. These companies and others like them choose their market niche and dominate it. They know that in order to grow as a business, they must compete and play to win. For these companies, second place is not part of their corporate culture.

---

*The Information Age creates significant obstacles*
*and opportunities for companies to compete and win*

---

 ### *Commitments are long-term*

There was a time when business deals were consummated with a handshake. Your word was your commitment and had lasting value. The speed of commerce today challenges the basic value of commitment. Worse, commitments are influenced by so many factors, that it is difficult at best to secure long-term commitments. The length of time for commitments is influenced by everything from the Internet to the whims of a chief executive officer and his or her relationship with the board of directors.

In professional football in the United States, there is a phrase called *Monday morning quarterbacking.* This is a time when fans, writers, coaches and players second-guess what transpired during competition on the previous weekend. The potential implications of Monday morning quarterbacking are that decisions can be made out of context and certainly in too-short timeframes. The New York Jets, a Super Bowl contender in 1998, were having a difficult start for the 1999 season. Expectations in the organiza-

166

tion were very high. The quarterback for the team was out for the season due to injury and the team was struggling. Their well-respected coach, Bill Parcells, made a statement about changes needing to be made! The players were nervous and the fans were calling for heads to roll.

One brave player, Keyshawn Johnson, an all-star wide receiver was asked about his perspective on the changes required. He responded that, *"our problem is an organization problem and starts at the top right down to the bottom. The players are only a part of our problem."* How refreshing! This player recognized that whatever problems the team was having, was a system problem and required a long-term commitment to success as opposed to a knee-jerk short-term reaction. There is no doubt in my mind that the coach of the Jets understands what it takes to build a winning franchise and was only trying to get his team to perform to its potential in the face of adversity.

This example, equally applies to business. You only have to replace the head coach with Chief Executive Officer and the fans, writers and executive management with shareowners, investors and analysts. Long-term commitments are a necessary condition for sustained success, and those companies that year in and year out meet or exceed shareowner expectations understand this requirement.

Long-term commitment, as a condition for success, does not mean investing money frivolously. It does not mean putting executives and employees in positions of responsibility beyond their ability. The issue of long-term commitment is as relevant in the hospitality industry as it is the communications industry. How many times do restaurants change ownership over and over again at a particular location? How many times have we seen start up companies or divisions within bigger companies, close down their business based on missed financial performance expectations? In the Information Age, the business opportunities are plentiful. The sheer volume of opportunities can prevent investors from completing due diligence before making their investment decisions. Business success has to be judged in context of the market environment and conditions required to be successful. Unfortunately, businesses often do not consider all aspects of their vision or strategy. Over time businesses make short-term decisions that undermine long-term commitments.

---

*Long-term commitments are required*
*for sustained business success*

---

 **The right people, at the right place, at the right time**

Another condition for success in *World's Best Value™* companies is people. Human resources have long been understood as a necessary ingredient for successful business outcomes. The challenge in the Information Age is to identify the right people. Many Fortune 500 companies go through periods of change that require their people to develop new skill sets and adapt to changing customer and market requirements. The same challenge exists in small to medium-sized companies as well. Time to market requirements do not allow companies the time to develop current employee skill sets.   Employees do not always have the desire or capacity to develop new skills.  In the Information Age, skill set shortages are common and represent a real threat to business growth.

*World's Best Value*™ companies are vigorously working on the human resource shortages that threaten their business growth.  On-line education is growing such that International Data Corp estimates the number of people taking undergraduate and graduate courses will increase to over two million in 2002, accounting for 15 percent of all higher-education students.

The next challenge is to have these trained human resources at the right place in order to create successful outcomes. Teleworking, telecommuting, video conferencing and teleconferencing help bridge time zone gaps and *virtually* apply people anywhere in the world.

*World's Best Value*™ companies often are multinational companies with business operations spread around the world. Air travel and the convergence of data communications and telecommunications provide tools for skilled people to bring value to their worldwide businesses and customers.  It is not just enough to have the right people; they have to be in the right place to be effective.

General Electric, Unisys, FedEx and Motorola, for example have corporate universities that give employees a mix of company culture, management skills and technical product training. Steve Kerr, General Electric's chief learning officer said in a *Business Week* interview that the goal is to give managers *"the ability to energize other people."* Corporate University Xchange Inc., a New York research and consulting firm estimates there are now over 1,600 such company-run universities in the United States.

Finally, time is an overlooked factor and is especially important in application of resources in the Information Age. Time is the great equalizer for business outcomes. An understanding of time dimensions in business decisions provides useful insight for risk analysis and scenario planning. If you believe in the *Chaos Theory,* you understand that nothing in the world happens accidentally. Often, successful business or personal outcomes are being in the right place at the right time. Good fortune and luck sometimes play a role in business, but good planning and creating the right conditions for success dramatically improve the odds for predictable success.

---

*Companies that put the right people in the right place at the right time have a greater likelihood of predictable business outcomes*

---

 ### Risk management and customer requirements

Business decisions are fundamentally the determination of return on resources within a defined tolerance of risk. The Internet and its borderless communication technologies is enabling a global financial transformation. The most dramatic impact on financial markets from the Internet we can anticipate is the efficient matching of investing and borrowing. Electronic risk management tools will become more widely available at lower costs for more people.

Siemens, the global networking conglomerate based in Munich, Germany, has a culture of assigning a commercial manager to every business unit manager in its business. The assumption is that a financially and commercially informed business manager will make better business decisions. The theory is outstanding, but one can imagine the inefficiencies if the information flow is not Internet real-time responsive communications. Siemens' centrally-based management decision hierarchy over time would not be competitive in a changing world. Siemens' challenge is to take this embedded culture and put its value on the corporate Intranet.

Everyone in the world has someone they are accountable to. All customers have their own customers and the environment is changing dramatically. Internet time demands timely decisions. I received a phone call recently from a logistics executive in a Fortune 500 company who was trying to clarify a particular point on a contract with my company. We were able to resolve the open issue, but what was interesting to me was that he immediately dialed my cell phone half way around the world, in order to get an answer and satisfy his customer's requirements. John Chambers of Cisco is well-known for keeping in contact around the clock with his worldwide sales force. He can be reached 24 hours a day, 7 days a week!

---

*Successful business outcomes require timely risk management decisions in order to meet customer requirements*

---

 ### Leadership is a science, in an art form

Leadership is a key ingredient to create ***World's Best Value™*** success. There has been so much written about the science of leadership. Consultants, writers and leaders often write about the characteristics of leadership styles and beliefs that work. They are able to articulate the specific attributes of successful leaders.

Not a lot has been written about the *soft science* or *art form* of leadership. There are exceptions, such as *Leadership is an Art* by *Max DuPree and The Tao of Leadership* by *John Heider*. These books, however, do not focus on the challenges and opportunities created by the Information Age. Leadership in the Information Age must consider Internet time. Leadership must consider communications in a distributed environment. Leadership must learn how to be personable using an impersonal e-mail system. Managing by walking around works if all of your people are in a single geographical location. It does not work as well if as a leader, you have responsibilities for people and businesses around the world.

The art of leadership in the Information Age must be more technologically sensitive. The use of technology in the workplace and the speed of change in general are increasing. Leaders must have confidence in their people and be adaptable to change. People are looking for a safe environment to take risks and make a difference in a marketplace characterized by turmoil and chaos.

172

## Create Conditions for Success

David Roussain, vice president for e-commerce and customer service at FedEx said in a *Business Week* interview that, *"an unbelievable amount of decisions are made over e-mail. It tends to push issues faster and quicker and allows for a freer exchange of opinions. It is also a safe environment to raise issues."* The art form of leadership here is to positively encourage risk taking and reinforce the failures and successes as learning and development opportunities.

We can all learn from industry leaders such as Bill Gates of Microsoft and Chris Galvin of Motorola who regularly communicate with every employee by e-mail and have an *open computer* policy. An open door policy is not enough in the Information Age.

---

*The Information Age demands artfully and scientifically applied leadership*

---

# *World's Best Value™* Plan
## Create Conditions for Success

Objective:  Create an environment for company success

Priorities:

1) Create a compete-to-win culture.

2) Be quick, nimble and fast.

3) Make a long-term commitment to success.

4) Do not undermine vision and strategy.

5) Put the right people in the right positions.

6) Understand time dimensions for decision-making.

7) Implement risk-analysis and scenario-planning disciplines.

8) Make timely and efficient risk management decisions.

9) Be responsive to customer requirements.

10) Apply leadership in an artful and disciplined manner.

# Chapter 13

## *World's Best Value™* Measurement Model

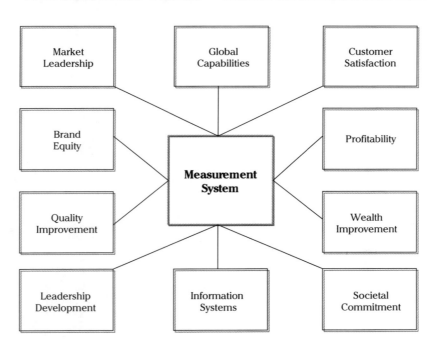

## World's Best Value™ Measurement Model

 ### Stakeholder indicators

A good way to measure **World's Best Value™** is to start with your stakeholders in the business. Stakeholders are customers, shareowners, employees and community. Each has a vested interested in a company's success and future. It makes a lot of sense to broaden the measurement of success beyond any one constituent. Each constituent is interdependent with the other and, accordingly, from a business perspective should be viewed as a system.

 ### Customers

There are numerous ways to measure customer satisfaction. The important learning from a **World's Best Value™** perspective is to view customer satisfaction as a whole. Customers will tell suppliers if they like their products and services by engaging in long-term buying relationships. Suppliers of products and services will always try to be responsive to their customer needs, but how does a company know if they are making progress in customer satisfaction? As mentioned earlier, the best companies in the world, measure a number of meaningful outcomes. The outcomes include on-time delivery, returned goods, increasing or decreasing levels of business, customer equipment uptime, satisfaction surveys and others. It is important to *blend* and *weight* these measurements with either subjective or objective criteria in order to base-line customer satisfaction, as a system, and measure improvement.

**Shareowners**

Investors in a business, or shareowners, have choices where to put their money. The best companies in the world understand that increasing shareowner value is an important outcome for long-term success. Increasing shareowner value provides public companies with currency to buy new businesses and expand operations. Increasing shareowner value provides *wealth creation based incentives* for employee stock option plans. The market share price or private investment share price is the measurement, and the share price must increase over time. The challenge for privately and publicly held companies is to refrain from short-term corrective actions based on tactical dynamics that do not relate to the underlying value of the business.

 **Employees**

The most popular tool for measuring employee satisfaction is surveys. The best companies use them and, at the same time, often get frustrated by them. Instead of using an employee survey as a learning opportunity to be better, some companies use them and become very introspective, if not paranoid. Employees are looking for a good job with a successful company that pays a fair wage for contributions provided. All of that is easy to say, but I've never met an employee who felt he or she was being fairly compensated.

The reasons range from what the employee needs to support a certain lifestyle to comparisons based on personalities with fellow employees. Another good measurement for employee satisfaction is attrition and employee turnover. I also like *revenues per employee* because it drives home the point of productivity as an important measurement for the business.

 ## *Community*

Two of the richest people in the world are Ted Turner, former founder of Cable News Network and Vice Chairman of Time Warner, and Bill Gates, Founder and Chief Executive Officer of Microsoft. Each has donated billions of dollars to charitable foundations and other causes, setting an example and standard for other people of wealth. People in many fine businesses around the world donate time, services and cash resources to charities and non-profit causes in their communities. Community involvement is very difficult to measure, but like everything, it is part of a system.

A blended measurement model can be created for community involvement as well. Absolute monies provided, employee time for company sponsored charity events and campaigns such as the United Way are good indicators of a company's involvement in its community. The one measurement that I particularly favor is the *matching-gift* program where a company donates an equal amount of money up to set limits for gift giving initiated by an individual. The reason I like matching-gifts so much is that it encourages employees to give where they like to give, apart from the company's interest. Matching-gift programs are a win-win-win for the recipient of the gift, employees and companies.

## World's Best Value™

 **World's Best Value™ indicators**

I have worked with and studied the business practices of small, medium and large companies around the world during the past two decades. AT&T, Cisco, Nortel, Lucent, General Electric, Ford and others have common characteristics that differentiate them from their global competitors. They consistently produce the best value in the world for their customers and are able to sustain success. Certain entrepreneurial businesses around the world including Atlantech, Paradyne, Sedona Networks, Cerent, Virata, Daleen Technologies and Redback Networks have displayed similar characteristics and are laying the foundations for *World's Best Value™* products and services. Following is a brief summary of those common characteristics that measure *World's Best Value™* for leading companies around the world:

---

*Business indicators are typically measured by* ***World's Best Value™*** *companies*

---

 *Market leadership*

There is a driving force within *World's Best Value™* companies to be a market leader in chosen market segments. The culture is relentless in measuring business plans, corporate strategies and performance related to market share. Many companies who do not achieve either first, second or third market share position in a growing market segment, should seriously consider exiting that business segment unless they can find a business model that sustains growth and profitability.

### World's Best Value™ Measurement Model

 **Global capabilities**

Leading companies in the world recognize that the global marketplace offers potential for business growth and success. These companies critically measure their ability to serve a particular market and determine the optimum business model for market success. ***World's Best Value™*** companies actively provide international development experiences for key executives and seek board members who have worldwide business experience.

 **Customer satisfaction index**

Not surprisingly, the best companies in the world measure customer satisfaction on a holistic system basis. They create a blend of meaningful customer measurements that reflect a critical look at what is most important to their customers. Toyota, Lucent, Cisco, Motorola and Nortel are some of the ***World's Best Value™*** companies that have developed and integrated customer satisfaction indexes for the business.

 **Brand awareness**

Companies that provide ***World's Best Value™*** products and services are fanatical about their company and product brands. Brand awareness is difficult to measure but often translate into a customer willingness to pay more for value, everything else being equal. We spoke earlier about the importance of branding and the value creation potential associated with brands. Coca-Cola, Disney, Microsoft and Sun Microsystems have very powerful global brands.

181

## TQM implementation

Total quality management is a cultural imperative in **World's Best Value**™ companies. The of quality improvement characterizes companies that breed TQM into their business processes. A blended series of measurements is a good way to look at TQM usage. For instance, on-time delivery across all business operations can measure implementation. Motorola, Lucent and IBM are particularly good in this area.

 ## Product and services quality

Product reliability, as measured by number of defects per million, is a good starting point for measuring product quality. Any measurement of defects related to transaction volume is typically used here. The Universal Card division of AT&T transformed the financial services industry in the early 1990s with its outstanding customer service. The challenge for financial service companies is to gain useful customer feedback in an environment where telephone solicitation is increasing significantly. A number of the hotel chains like Hilton are doing some very good work in this area with their 60-second feedback form.

 ## Leadership development

Measurement of leadership development is normally based on training experiences and developmental assignments. International assignments, turn around business opportunities and new business creation responsibilities are particularly good for leadership development. *Business Week* reported that Intel actively encourages its managers to switch jobs and in 1998, about 10 percent of Intel's staff of 67,000 changed jobs within the company. Intel has to be fluid and operate at hyper-speed with six-month product cycles. ***World's Best Value™*** companies place an extremely high emphasis on leadership development and actively create opportunities to develop their brightest and talented employees. General Electric, AT&T, Intel, Dell and Coca-Cola are well recognized in the area of leadership development.

 ### *Corporate strategy execution*

The best measurement for execution of corporate strategy is financial performance against plan. Employee visibility and understanding of corporate strategy is another useful way to ensure the key elements of corporate strategy are integrated across the organization. I have found this measurement to be lacking in most companies because they fear a breach of confidentiality. Corporate strategy is sometimes thought to be the privileged knowledge of a few. There needs to be a way to translate corporate strategy to execution. In my experience, the ***World's Best Value™*** planning tool or measurements against company priorities are a good place to start.

 ### *World-class information systems*

This is a *difference maker* in the Information Age. The Internet enables instantaneous decision-making. Timely information can result in productivity and customer satisfaction. There can and should be much debate on the optimum information system network, but the key measurement is ease of use and usefulness of information for customers and employees. Electronic commerce and electronic data interchange are essential information systems used by *World's Best Value*™ companies. As mentioned earlier, Cisco is pioneering the implementation of a virtual closing of its financial records on a demand-driven basis.

 ## *Societal Commitment*

Societal commitment is a difficult one to measure. *World's Best Value*™ companies accept their social responsibilities and give back to the communities in which they operate. They strive to work in harmony with the environment. Companies such as Kennecot, International Paper, Philip Morris, Enron, Dupont and Exxon, find it very challenging to find the right balance of growing a profitable business, creating shareowner wealth and protecting the environment. The key measurement here is a company's willingness to take a leadership role in working in harmony with regulatory authorities, often resulting in the creation of new cost-effective technologies that protect the environment.

 ## *Profitability*

Sustained profitability creates cash for investments in growth opportunities. It is probably the most important measurement. Businesses cannot sustain themselves without profit. This is not always obvious in start-up Internet companies, but keep in mind that planned losses can be acceptable if balanced by future growth and profitability. General Electric, IBM and Microsoft are profit-making machines that produce *World's Best Value™* products and services.

 ## Wealth creation

The creation of wealth for shareowners is a source of capital that enables businesses to grow and sustain profitability. The Information Age creates new business models for companies and industries. Widespread use of the Internet and resulting electronic commerce is expected to increase global gross domestic product by up to one percent early in the next century.

---

*World's Best Value™ companies have performance characteristics that can be measured*

---

# World's Best Value™ Plan
## World's Best Value™ Measurement Model

Objective: Establish measurement system for *World's Best Value™*

Priorities:

1) Measure market leadership relative to competition.

2) Critically assess and improve global capabilities.

3) Develop a customer satisfaction index.

4) Create and measure brand identity.

5) Establish and measure quality improvement.

6) Create a leadership development program.

7) Implement world-class information systems.

8) Work in harmony with communities.

9) Widely implement profitability targets.

10) Create wealth improvement index for shareholders.

# Chapter 14

# The Bar Just Got Higher

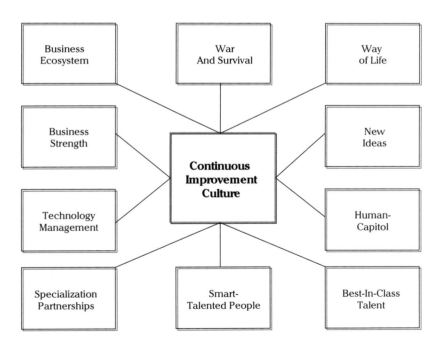

Business Ecosystem

War And Survival

Way of Life

Business Strength

New Ideas

Technology Management

Continuous Improvement Culture

Human-Capitol

Specialization Partnerships

Smart-Talented People

Best-In-Class Talent

## The Bar Just Got Higher

 *It's war and survival*

Jim Moore, the highly talented and intellectual founder of GEO Partners, describes business as an ecosystem that is as much a part of business creation as corporate survival. I like to think about business competition in the context of military analogies such as battles, wars, victories and defeats. We hear the same kind of thinking and expressions in athletic competition.

It is important for companies that provide *World's Best Value™* products and services to understand their competitors are trying to put them out of business. A culture of invincibility can lead to arrogance and insularity. It is better to run scared even if the competition is not right behind you. The Information Age has created an Internet environment where the barriers to entry in most industries are relatively low.

Success can create a competitive environment of war-like proportions. In the communications industry it is recognized that Cisco, Lucent and Nortel compete vigorously and have a strong respect and often dislike for each other. What else should we expect from the three market leaders in the fastest growing marketplace in the world?

War can bring out the best and worst in people and companies. It can create an environment of fear and apprehension and at the same time, strength and courage. A key learning from global competition is that customer expectations of price-quality-value benefits continuously increase. Customers have choices, and not everyone in a chosen industry segment will be successful. Further, lack of sustained growth and success ultimately means business atrophy or death. The stakes are high and global competition is truly about business survival.

---

*The bar keeps getting higher for global competitors who*
*recognize success is a matter of business survival*

---

 ### Continuous improvement — a way of life

*"Only the strong survive."* I remember hearing these words when I was a young man and never realized how profound the statement is. As we experience life and living, we learn that everything in the universe, including business, is a system. Is it overwhelming or inspirational to know that every day we must be better than the previous day if we are to compete and survive? The answer to the question of survival and continuous improvement is complex. For me, it boils down to the capacity of people and businesses. If the capacity of the human spirit is unlimited, then continuous improvement is an opportunity to be strong and get better. If the human spirit is limited, then continuous improvement is bounded.

Business can learn a lot from the law of the jungle and the nature of ecosystems. I was fishing on the West Coast of Florida recently with my sons, Joe, Tommy and several of their friends. We were fishing for snook, which can be a very lively and challenging fishing experience. As we were casting our live bait, we noticed that several snook were coming in from the Gulf of Mexico into an inlet where smaller fish were present. The snook began a feeding frenzy. It occurred to me at that time, the purpose of fish in an ecosystem is to feed off each other.

No sooner did we observe the snook coming into the inlet then we noticed a porpoise swimming easily into the inlet as well. The porpoise, just as quickly, disappeared from our sight, but it was exciting to see such a large mammal swimming in the water. The next moment we hooked a snook and the contest was underway. Unfortunately, almost instantly thereafter, the porpoise grabbed the snook and started carrying the three-foot, thirty-pound snook off to the gulf. We had just witnessed the ecosystem at work!

It is not different from business. Companies must continuously improve their business or they don't survive. It might take months or years before it is absorbed or bankrupt, but inevitably it happens. The notion of continuous improvement can be foreign to many people. That is not the case with **World's Best Value™** companies. These businesses do not fret about changes in the marketplace, they embrace them. They do not worry about declining prices; they reduce their costs even further. They do not react to new business environments; they proactively create the environment they want. The key is to embrace change and keep getting better.

---

*Continuous improvement is an essential business
culture and enables the strong to survive*

---

191

**Smaller, faster, cheaper**

Advances in communications, computing, digital signal processor and microelectronic technologies are changing everything in business. The life cycle of new products in the Information Age will be measured in months and time-to-market advantage decreases as markets mature and develop. In addition, miniaturization technologies used in the consumer electronics industry are being applied to the communications industry. The continuous advancement and improvement in these technologies result in products that are smaller, faster and cheaper.

The key implication for businesses in the Information Age is that the management of technology is becoming a science. It is a complex business-risk when technology shifts have the capacity to cannibalize entire product lines. Product roadmaps are a necessity and the science of scenario planning must be applied to deal with the uncertainties of changing customer requirements and technology shifts.

Just about every major corporation in the world has a senior executive in charge of Internet technology. At General Motors, the title is e-Vice President. Companies who want to consistently provide **World's Best Value™** products and services must stay ahead of technology trends. Declining product margins will be the outcome for those companies that do not anticipate smaller, faster and cheaper product requirements.

Specialization of business functions is required in order to consistently create outcomes of smaller, faster and cheaper products. In the information technologies industry, for example, owning a factory can be a liability. Hewlett Packard, IBM, Sun, Motorola, Cisco, Nortel and others extensively use contract manufacturers such as Solectron, Flextronics and SCI Systems.

The resulting alliances enable each business function to specialize and optimize business outcomes. Costs are significantly reduced as a result of worldwide manufacturing across numerous companies and industries.

---

*Electronic, miniaturization and manufacturing technologies enable products to be produced smaller, faster and cheaper*

---

 ### Draft choices, free agents and franchise players

How do the best companies in the world stay ahead of their competitors in an environment of increasing competition and continuous improvement? They look at the development of human capital as critically important. *Fortune Magazine* reported in 1999 that Michael Dell, founder of Dell Computer, made people the number one priority on his list of top 10 most important things at his company. Companies like Dell cannot get enough smart, talented, hard-working people to execute their business strategies.

Leading companies such as Intel, Cisco and America On Line are either acquiring talent through acquisition or establishing tightly coupled relationships with universities to create a flow of new talent into their companies. At Cisco, for instance, the culture is very competitive and demanding. Employees are expected to produce outcomes according to plan. If Cisco employees do not produce, the employees are just as likely to be replaced or given opportunities to contribute somewhere else in the company. Andersen Consulting, McKinsey, KPMG and other public accounting, auditing and consulting firms are well known for creating similar results-oriented environments.

As long as the demand for talented people exceeds supply, opportunities for wealth creation abound. Premiums are paid for top technical and executive leadership talent in particular. In addition, bonus and retention schemes for top performers make it very difficult for these employees to leave a successful growing business. Internet companies such as Brainbuzz.com, Monster.com and others are pioneering on-line recruiting practices.

*Business Week* reported that Bob Herbold, Microsoft's executive vice president and chief operating officer said his company's number one competency is recruiting. *"We are after smart folks who are fired up about improving people's lives via software, no matter where they live."* Almost 40 percent of Microsoft new-hires come from referrals. Cisco favors building a culture that wants people from different backgrounds and environments. A large percentage of Cisco employees were acquired through acquisition. Brainpower is what counts. Cisco has a culture that thrives on acceptance of new ideas and people.

Internet time has paved the path for Internet recruiting. It becomes a numbers game for the thousands of recruiters who are feverishly staffing companies in the Information Age. Many companies are reporting a more personalized recruiting process because of the interaction of e-mail. The time from application to offer has shortened as well.

---

*Investment in human capital is a priority for*
*leading companies in the Information Age*

---

# *World's Best Value*™ **Plan**
## The Bar Just Got Higher

Objective:  Create a continuous improvement culture.

Priorities:

1)  Think of business as part of an ecosystem.

2)  Embrace competition in terms of war and survival.

3)  Make continuous improvement a way of life.

4)  Make continuous improvement a business strength.

5)  Manage technology for continuous improvement.

6)  Develop specialization partnerships.

7)  Hire smart, talented people.

8)  Recruit best-in-class talent from industry leaders.

9)  Create a culture that thrives on new ideas.

10) Invest in human-capital.

# Chapter 15

## In Pursuit of *World's Best Value™*

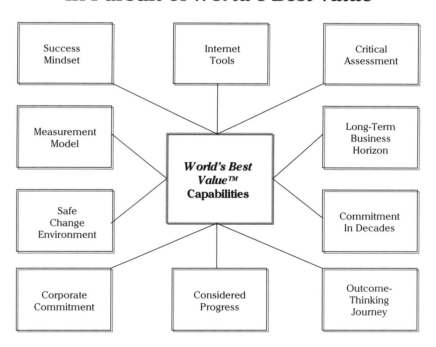

## In Pursuit of World's Best Value™

 ### So you want to be the best

For many people and companies, it is a bit overwhelming to think about doing the things required to be the best. Many employees and businesses are quite happy with their lot in life with no intention of pursuing **World's Best Value™**. The thought of developing strategy, market leadership, personal leadership, quality practices, branding and global thinking may be overwhelming. The passion is not present.

For those who may not want to take up the **World's Best Value™** mantle, it is only a matter of time before the consequences of inaction catches up with you and your business.

**World's Best Value™** does not just exist in large multinational or global companies. **World's Best Value™** may be around the corner or down the street. It was not that long ago when family hardware stores were the norm in the United States. Little did these proprietors realize that Home Depot and Lowe's had a vision of countrywide market leadership in the home building supplies business? How about the local cinema in your favorite downtown area? These 1 and 2 screen cinemas are being wiped out as fast as AMC movie theatres and others can build their 20-screen entertainment complexes.

The Internet is changing the retail industry as we know it. Businesses must build distribution competitive advantage through personalized service in addition to a very focused electronic commerce system. If a business is going to focus only on face-to-face service, they need to be very focused on small market niches that are not going to be served by electronic commerce.

## World's Best Value™

Being the best has to start at the very top of any organization. There has to be a passion of vision and capacity to compete with the best companies in the world. Pursuing **World's Best Value™** takes years to accomplish. It is a *tough but rewarding journey*. My suggestion is to be honest with yourself and your business before you get started. It is the only way to begin.

---

*People and businesses that pursue*
***World's Best Value™** must want to be the best*

---

 ### Critical assessment of where you are

The first step in pursuit of **World's Best Value™** is to take off the rose-colored glasses and critically assess your business before you start on the journey. Sometimes a third party can help with the process of critical assessment. The challenge here is to trust the third party and be open to learning and understanding. This is difficult for most businesses.

Professional athletics is actually an easier model given the widespread availability of statistics on individual and team performance. Videotapes are available to judge competition against teams on any given day. Businesses struggle with this direct feedback. While businesses may understand its competition, a critical independent assessment of competition is generally not available.

A good place to begin the critical assessment is to measure your business against the criteria in the **World's Best Value™** *mea-*

*surement model.* Market leadership, global capabilities, customer satisfaction index, brand awareness, TQM implementation, product and service quality, leadership development, corporate strategy execution, world-class information systems, commitment to society and wealth creation can all be measured. If your business is either a start-up or relatively new company, it is perfectly acceptable to create an arbitrary rank order measurement system to get started.

For instance each of the measurements can have a 1-5 low to excellent ranking or A-F grade ranking. Keep in mind that the more specific the ranking the more useful it is to your business and future measurements. *However, the key is to get started.* So many businesses never begin the journey because they are unable to measure and get started. What a shame!

Initially, it is important to create a safe environment for self-analysis and critical assessment. If the anticipated results are expected to be poor, the worst thing that can happen is for employees to look over their shoulders and be concerned only about their own individual contributions to the business. A large part of **World's Best Value™** is the underlying processes in the business that enable sustainable and predictable business results. If there is an indictment to be made at the beginning of the critical assessment, it must start with the top leadership in a business, but even then, it should quickly subside based on the bravery, character and leadership required to move forward.

---

*People and companies must critically assess*
*their business to benchmark the starting point*
*for pursuit of **World's Best Value™***

---

 ***Shared corporate commitment for the race***

Individual initiative is not enough to pursue ***World's Best Value™***. The entire system, including employees, management and the board of directors must be committed. Eventually human energy will fail if there is not support from all perspectives within the business. It is important to keep in mind that the pursuit of ***World's Best Value™*** promises the future of your business to be bright, full of sustained profitability and growth. It is a worthwhile pursuit.

I like to think of business development and change management initiatives in terms of running a high hurdle race. In a high hurdle race, typically over a distance of 100, 200 and 400 meters, the runners step up to the starting line with a number of hurdles to cross before reaching the finish line. In a high hurdle race, the runners have every intention to finish the race. There are obstacles (hurdles) along the way. Athletes are trained to have the capacity and stamina to run the race with passion and vigor.

The same is true in pursuit of ***World's Best Value™***. The key is to make a decision to run the race. The decision to run the race must be supported by all parts of the business, otherwise the personal and professional risks are too great. Just because a person or business runs the race, there is no guarantee that they will finish. There is also no guarantee that the person or company will decide, while in the race, to cross the next hurdle. Thinking of the pursuit of **World's Best Value™** in this manner breaks the race down into smaller parts, which makes it a bit less intimidating.

Like a good project plan, there should be visibility to all of the hurdles and requirements to cross the finish, *before* the race is started. It is a very simple concept with profound consequences. Do not run the high hurdle race unless there is shared corporate commitment, otherwise the journey will inevitably fail.

---

*The pursuit of **World's Best Value™** requires a shared corporate commitment in order to begin and sustain the journey*

---

 ### Time can be measured in decades

Maybe the Asians as a culture best understand time and perspectives about time. It is not unusual for Asian companies to think about their businesses in 10-year horizons. American businesses do not usually contemplate their business or strategy in such time frames. I have worked with and observed numerous businesses that can think no further than monthly and quarterly financial results. Not surprisingly, these are the kind of companies that are often gripped in the vice of survival. Short-term thinking companies often find it very difficult to break the cycle of short-term results versus long-term strategy and sustained business results.

## World's Best Value™

Do you think that Microsoft, General Motors or IBM have long term plans? Do these companies, and other market leaders like them, have a view about long-term consumer purchasing and technology trends that may affect their business? Are **World's Best Value™** companies thinking about planned product obsolescence and determining the financial impact on their business? We can be certain **World's Best Value™** companies with world-class product development cycle times have a long-term view of their businesses.

The pursuit of **World's Best Value™** is not going to happen over night. It takes years and often decades to be certain that your business is among the best in the world at what it does. The time frame can certainly be shorter for smaller businesses. Ideally, the new companies born in the Information Age such as America on Line, Amazon.com and Yahoo are building their business for sustained **World's Best Value™**. One of the remaining legacies that Jack Welch, chief executive officer, of General Electric wants to leave before he retires, is a company that is built on the foundation and principles that is really the sum total of **World's Best Value™**. He wants to ensure that total quality management is internalized throughout the business. He wants to make sure his industry record of quarter-over-quarter revenue and profit growth is sustained.

---

*The pursuit of **World's Best Value™** is a long-term commitment and can take decades to achieve*

---

# *World's Best Value*™ **Plan**
## In Pursuit of *World's Best Value*™

Objective: Actively pursue *World's Best Value*™ capabilities.

Priorities:

1) Embrace the fear of success.

2) Actively engage the Internet as a business tool.

3) Critically assess the starting position.

4) Measure business against the *World's Best Value*™ model.

5) Create a safe environment for assessment and self-analysis.

6) Ensure shared corporate commitment for the race.

7) Consider progress in terms of a high-hurdle race.

8) Begin the journey with the end in mind.

9) Think in terms of 10-year business horizons.

10) Make long-term commitments measured in decades.

# Chapter 16

## You Can Change the World

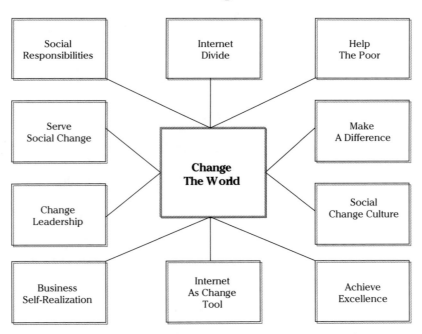

Social Responsibilities

Internet Divide

Help The Poor

Serve Social Change

Make A Difference

**Change The World**

Change Leadership

Social Change Culture

Business Self-Realization

Internet As Change Tool

Achieve Excellence

## You Can Change the World

 *Social responsibilities of World's Best Value™ companies*

**World's Best Value™** companies are privileged. They are unique and different to most other companies in the world. They have worked hard to secure a leadership position in their industry and at the same time they are blessed to have such a responsibility. We have all heard about people in every industry who have said, *"I never wanted to be a role model."*

It has only been within the past several years that Bill Gates of Microsoft accepted his social responsibilities of being the richest man in the world running one of the most powerful and successful companies on the planet. He and his family are reaching out to the less fortunate. By giving to social initiatives such as access to the Internet for low-income communities, vaccination for needy children, maternal mortality, malaria and AIDS vaccination, Bill Gates and his foundation are finding the right mix of social responsibilities and business passion.

Business and government leaders are stepping up to their responsibilities. Bill Bradley, the respected former U.S. senator, professional basketball player and Rhodes Scholar is promoting ideas to feed starving children and provide medical coverage for the poor and less fortunate in the United States. His perspectives, in my view, are not about political affiliation, Democrat, Republican or Reform Party, but rather social responsibilities. The political mechanics for such causes can and should be debated.

Further, as the Internet spreads throughout the world, many believe it will only continue to drive a wedge between the rich and poor, the have and have-nots. We are just beginning to see some of the statistics on this issue. In America, dividing lines are showing up based on race, income and education. The commerce department and census bureau report that three times as many Caucasians have Internet access compared to Blacks and Hispanics. Households with incomes of $75,000 dollars or more have ten times the Internet access compared to incomes of less than $15,000 dollars. College graduates have three times the Internet access compared to high school graduates and ten times those with elementary education.

It is good business to give back to your community and society. There must be cooperation between business and governments on a wide range of socioeconomic issues. In a global capitalist society, it is unhealthy and politically unstable for people, businesses and countries to leave the less fortunate and needy behind in the Information Age. People connected to the Internet, transacting business, sharing ideas and instantly communicating with each other, can make a tremendous social impact. The Information Age has the potential to bring people together and create worldwide economic prosperity.

---

*World's Best Value*™ *companies have the greatest potential and social responsibility to lead the worldwide Information Age revolution*

---

## You Can Change the World

 ### The best keep getting better

The best companies and people in the world are motivated to continuously improve. Shareowners, customers, employees and communities expect sustained excellence. Bobby Bowden, the legendary head football coach of Florida State University, was asked in 1993 if he thought he would lose the championship drive after winning his first National Championship. He replied winning was better than losing and it was time to focus on winning a second championship. If you know Bobby Bowden, you know his comment had nothing to do with pride, ego or greed. It had to do with his responsibilities as a head football coach to his players, athletic department, university and alumni. For he and his coaching staff, football is a ministry to provide an environment for talented student-athletes to be the best they can be.

Similar stories can be told about the leading companies in the world who continually raise the bar to improve and sustain their leadership position in the market. Serving social needs does not necessarily drive **World's Best Value™** performance. However, social and corporate needs are interdependent.

Critical mass also has something to do with the best getting better. The size and scale of businesses can be an advantage in terms of growing a profitable business. This can be as true with large global businesses as it is with smaller companies focused on niche markets. We have all heard the term, *"success breeds success."* Success has so many positive implications for human motivation and individual or business self-realization. The concept of *fulfillment* is a key driver behind the best getting better.

209

*Individual and business self-realization*
*drive the best to keep getting better*

 ### Reaching out for social change

The Information Age is spawning worldwide growth as profoundly as the invention of electricity and railroads. Availability and manipulation of information increasingly replace the traditional economic factors of capital resources and skilled labor that historically underpins growth.

When new technologies appear, the social consequences are not always readily apparent. The internal combustion engine, electric power, telephone, television, microelectronics, computing technologies and the Internet are changing the fabric of society. Social scientists will write about the social impact from the Information Age in the years to come. There will be significant social change in the future.

*World's Best Value™* companies are ideally positioned to reach out and lead the social change, far greater than governments that feel the effect of change caused by industry. Government can create public policy that takes advantage of technology, but it cannot do it independently from the source. Leading by example has never been so essential.

*World's Best Value™ companies are ideally*
*positioned to reach out and lead the social changes*
*resulting from the Information Age*

## You Can Change the World

 *If you're not changing the world, you're taking up space!*

***World's Best Value***™ is all about passion, learning, development, quality, leadership, strategy, information systems and customer satisfaction. It is about doing the things that customers value the most. ***World's Best Value***™ companies are unique compared to their competitors. They are driven to achieve excellence. They have a sense of social responsibility that transcends their business. They are trying to make a difference in the world, relative to their position in the marketplace.

Dr. James Gill, the renowned eye surgeon and triathlete, founded a business in Tarpon Springs, Florida, called St. Lukes Cataract Eye Clinic. My experience with his business was nothing short of world-class. The passion, quality, leadership and attention to customer satisfaction were evident throughout the clinic. Employees had state-of-the-art information systems, medical equipment and world-class business process systems. The experience was one of the best medical and business experiences I have ever encountered. ***World's Best Value***™ can show up anywhere.

Physics helps us understand that a planted tree living in an environment of no wind will weaken and fall over. Wind places a resistance on the tree that actually makes the tree stronger. Change, or wind, in this instance, makes things stronger. The same is true for people and businesses. *Change should be welcomed with open arms.* Problems are to be accepted as opportunities for improvement. Issues are nothing more than events to be overcome.

Not everyone in the world can be a leader. Nor can every business be the best at what they do in a globally competitive marketplace. We have a choice to lead or follow. We have a choice to be proactive or reactive. We have a choice to be at the forefront of social change. We have a choice to create sustained business success for stakeholders. With knowledge of our choices, we have a responsibility to choose *World's Best Value*™.

I like to think in terms of human ergs of energy. Each of us has a defined number of days, months or years remaining on the planet. We must choose to grab hold of our human and business potential and make changes that create *World's Best Value*™. If we are not changing the world, we are taking up space!

---

*The capacity of the human spirit is unlimited and we can choose to create* ***World's Best Value***™

---

# *World's Best Value™* Plan
## You Can Change the World

Objective:  Accept the social responsibilities of being *World's Best Value™*

Priorities:

1) Embrace business passion with social responsibilities.

2) Close the Internet divide between have and have-nots.

3) Help the poor who are left behind in the Information Age.

4) Manage business results to include serving social change.

5) Lead social change by example.

6) Embrace success for *business self-realization*.

7) Use the Internet to positively change the fabric of society.

8) Achieve excellence and make a difference in the world.

9) Welcome change as an opportunity for making a difference.

10) Always think in terms of changing the world.

# Suggested Readings

- Business 2.0 Magazine

- Business Week Magazine

- Competing for the Future
    Gary Hamel & C.K. Prahalad

- Financial Times

- Fortune Magazine

- Global Paradox
    John Naisbitt

- How World-Class Companies Became World-Class
    Cuno Pumpin

- Investors Business Daily

- Ishmael, An Adventure of the Mind and Spirit
    Daniel Quinn

- Kaizen – The Key to Japan's Competitive Success
    Masaaki Imai

- Leadership Jazz
    Max DePree

- On Becoming a Leader
    Warren Bennis

## Suggested Readings

- Principle Centered Leadership
    Stephen R. Covey

- Red Herring Magazine

- Rethinking the Future
    Rowan Gibson

- The Discipline of Market Leaders
    Michael Treacy & Fred Wiersema

- The Fifth Discipline, The Art and Practice of the
  Learning Organization
    Peter M. Senge

- The Seven Habits of Highly Effective People
    Stephen R. Covey

- The World in 2020
    Hamish McRae

- Total Global Strategy, Managing for Worldwide Competitive
  Advantage
    George Yip

- Total Quality Management In Action
    Howard & Shelly Gitlow

- Wall Street Journal

# Index

216

# Index

# Index

Investech Foundation, 135
Investment,
    10, 22, 25, 26, 29, 30, 31, 33, 36,
    37, 41, 46, 47, 48, 52, 63, 65, 76,
    104, 128, 133, 134, 168, 178, 184,
    195
ISDN, 51

## J

J.C. Penney, 73
Jaguar, 6, 42
Japan,
    12, 40, 47, 85, 103, 108, 110, 139,
    157, 214
Jewish, 145
Johnson and Johnson, 94, 95
Johnson, Keyshawn, 167
Joint venture, 52, 128

## K

K-Mart, 73
Kaizen, 110, 112, 214
Kerr, Steve, 169
KPMG, 194

## L

Latin American, xviii, 52, 98
Law of absorption, 131
Law of diminishing returns,
    41, 147, 149
Law of increasing returns,
    147, 148, 149
Leadership is an art, 172
Lexus, 60, 73, 121, 122
Livermore, Ann, 84
London Business School, 43
Low cost, 10, 11, 35, 76
Low cost values, 11, 12
Lowe's, 122, 199
Lucent Technologies,
    xii, 37, 77, 131, 137

## M

Macoby, Michael, 126
Major league baseball, 136
Manchester United, 45, 138
Market leadership,
    51, 53, 54, 56, 57, 59, 60, 61, 64,
    65, 66, 133, 137, 141, 180, 186,
    199, 201
Maslow's hierarchy of needs, 134
Matching-gift program , 179
McDonald's, 23, 54, 57
MCIWorldCom, xv, xvii, 42
McGinn, Rich, xii, 37, 147
McKinsey, 8, 194
Media One, 23
Megatrends Asia, 34
Mentoring, 62
Mentors, xi, 62
Merck, 23
Microelectronic technologies, 192
Microsoft,
    xii, xvii, 14, 27, 29, 33, 57, 87, 93,
    119, 134, 148, 173, 179, 181, 185,
    194, 204, 207
Millennium, 5, 93
Miniaturization technologies, 192
Monday morning quarterbacking,
    166
Moore, Jim, 189
Motorola,
    xii, xvi, 12, 51, 77, 105, 110, 115,
    131, 155, 156, 169, 173, 181, 182,
    193
Multinational,
    17, 21, 22, 30, 52, 99, 125, 169,
    199
Murdoch, Rupert, 21, 45
Muslim, 145

## N

Naisbitt, John, 14, 34, 214

219

# Index

## W

Waitrose, 123
Wal-Mart, 64, 76, 122, 123, 166
Wall Street, 23, 93, 215
Wall Street Journal, 74
Wang, 10
Warner-Lambert, 27
Wealth creation 178, 185, 194, 201
Welch, Jack,
   xii, 21, 58, 97, 107, 143, 204
Wendy's 54
Westell, xii, 17, 69, 103
Woods, Tiger, 138
World Cup, 136
World Trade Organization, 34
World Wrestling Federation, 44
World-class,
   xv, xvi, xvii, xviii, 4, 6, 7, 8, 15, 18,
   37, 55, 60, 63, 66, 71, 76, 77, 79,
   80, 88, 103, 104, 105, 146, 153,
   204, 211
World-class information systems,
   183, 186, 201
World's largest industry, 4, 41, 42

## Y

Yahoo, xii, xviii, 93, 120, 155, 204
Yang, Jerry, xii

## Z

Zero defects, 105